ROME

Granta City Guides

ROME

ELIZABETH SPELLER

Granta Books

London

Granta Publications, 2/3 Hanover Yard, Noel Road, London N1 8BE

First published in Great Britain by Granta Books 2005

A CIP catalogue record for this book
is available from the British Library.

1 3 5 7 9 10 8 6 4 2

Typeset by M Rules

Printed and bound in Italy by Legoprint

CONTENTS

My thanks go to Mary Beard, Michael Bywater, Georgina Capel, Alberto Cherubini, Catharine Edwards, David Hawkins, Karen Hore, Dr Jim Hutchinson, Christopher Kelly, Lorna McNeur, George Miller, Daniel Morneau, Graham Palmer, Daniela Petrou, Katharine Reeve, Jeremy Speller, Caroline Vout and Tim Wright. Their guidance, criticism, contributions and, above all, love and understanding of Rome have made a dauntingly unbounded project more manageable. I am indebted to the indefatigable Howard and Anne Hyman and to Catherine and John Hopkins who were, in effect, my guinea pigs, trying out these walks during a Roman heatwave.

I am also grateful to The British School at Rome and to Lucy Cavendish College, Cambridge, where I held a Visiting Scholarship in 2004 which enabled me to work on this book.

To my daughter, Miranda

Stendhal's syndrome (sten.DAWLZ sin.drum, -drohm) *n.* Dizziness, panic, paranoia or madness caused by viewing certain artistic or historical artifacts or by trying to see too many such artifacts in too short a time. Identified in 1970 by Dr Graziella Magherini, chief of psychiatry at Florence's Santa Maria Nuova Hospital.

Novembre:

Dei giovani e dei Vecchi
si reggruppano
fra le rovine calde di Roma,
se cui I platani lasciano cadere
con rumore di carta
le loro foglie dorate.
I giovani
quello che a loro piace,
e I Vecchi fanno finta di non sentire.

November:

Young folks and old folks
form their little groups
among the hot ruins of Rome,
on which the plane-trees drop
with paper sounds
their golden leaves.
The young let the old know
just what they like,
and the old pretend that they don't care.

From Aldo Palazzeschi, *Viaggio Sentimentale* (1955)

A BRIEF HISTORY
OF ROME

1480	Lucrezia Borgia, daughter of the future Pope Alexander VI, born
1483	The artist Raphael born
1525	The composer Palestrina born
1527	Rome sacked by troops of Emperor Charles V
1564	Michelangelo dies aged 89
1599	Noblewoman Beatrice Cenci beheaded for murdering her father
1600	Philosopher Giordano Bruno executed for heresy
17th cent.	**Rome is artistic capital of Europe**
1680	Sculptor and architect Gian Lorenzo Bernini dies
1751	Giovanni Battista Piranesi publishes *Veduta di Roma* (Views of Rome)
1788	Johann Wolfgang von Goethe finishes *Italian Journey*
1797	Napoleon captures Rome
1816	Gioacchino Rossini's *Barber of Seville* (*Almaviva*) has its disastrous premiere in Rome
1821	Poet John Keats dies at his house by the Spanish Steps
1822	Poet Percy Bysshe Shelley drowns at Livorno and is buried in Rome
1848	Rise of nationalists who declare a Republic; pope flees
1849	Pope returns under protection of the French
1860	*The Golden Faun* by Nathaniel Hawthorne published
1870	**Royalist troops take Rome; Italy is unified**
1871	*Middlemarch* by George Eliot published
1879	*Daisy Miller* by Henry James published
1922	Mussolini becomes Prime Minister
1929	The Vatican becomes a separate state

1940	Italy joins Second World War as member of Axis powers
1943	Germans occupy Rome after Italy surrenders to the Allies; Princess Mafalda of Savoy sent to Buchenwald Concentration Camp where she dies in 1944
1944	Allies liberate Rome
1946	Royal family sent into exile
1953	The film *Roman Holiday*, with Gregory Peck and Audrey Hepburn, released
1958	Italy joins European Common Market
1960	Frederico Fellini's film *La Dolce Vita* released
1969	Frederico Fellini's film *Satyricon* released
1978	Murder of politician Aldo Moro by Red Brigades
1982	Italy wins football World Cup
1982	Banco Ambrosiano scandal
1985	Terrorists kill sixteen at Rome airport
1993	Mafia bombings of two churches in Rome
1993	Silvio Berlusconi founds new political party Forza Italia

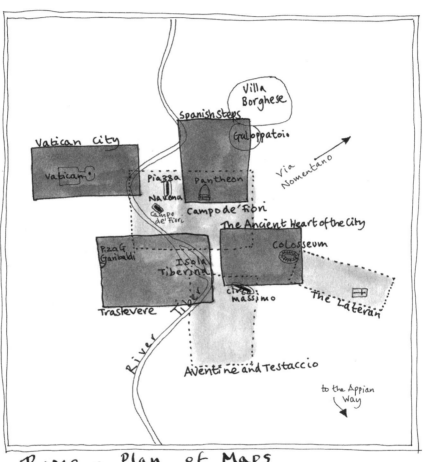

Villa Borghese

Spanish Steps

Galoppatoio

Vatican City

Vaticano

Piazza Navona

Pantheon

Campo de' Fiori

Campo de' Fiori

Via Nomentano

The Ancient Heart of the City

Pza G Garibaldi

Isola Tiberina

Colosseum

Trastevere

Circo Massimo

The Lateran

River Tiber

Aventine and Testaccio

to the Appian Way

Rome ~ Plan of Maps

INTRODUCTION

For anyone more familiar with the great capitals of northern Europe, Rome comes as a surprise. For a start it lacks the formality and relative uniformity of style that characterize central London or Paris. To an outsider Rome feels more like a relaxed provincial city. It has none of the late nineteenth-century planned expansion of many European cities; Rome's broadest boulevards are those imposed by Mussolini in the 1930s. Instead, perfectly modern lives continue in medieval streets, lanes and tiny piazzas. In place of the cool grey monumentalism of other capital cities, Rome basks in a certain fading, flaking, and ultimately finely calculated, neglect. Warm shades of terracotta and ochre soften even the harshest winter's day. By night, its streets deliberately under-lit, Romans must be some of the few city-dwellers in the world who can still look up and see the stars.

The city founded on seven hills is also a city of wonderful views; the Pincio, the Janiculum and the Aventine all spread Rome before you and, beyond it, the mountains, capped with snow in winter, hazy on the hottest summer's day. Start and end at one of these viewpoints and much that is otherwise incomprehensible may be understood.

The sounds of Rome are the sounds of vespas puttering, the roar of traffic as the lights change, of café chatter, the thin ringing of bells in the *campanili*, pigeons and the shouts of market traders. Tangled together in delectable visual chaos are the fragments of imperial Rome, the fortified towers and narrow alleys of the Middle Ages, the great baroque façades of hundreds of churches built at the height of papal supremacy, the numerous flower-filled balconies and terraces, the old tiles of different roof levels (many illegal additions), and modern offices, bars and shops designed with typically Italian panache. Dig down anywhere in central Rome and you will almost certainly find significant archaeological remains; indeed simply descend to many private cellars. It is why the underground train system is so limited. These different ages of Rome are not neatly arranged layer upon layer; instead they burst forth: the head of a 2000-year-old column strangely marooned in a medieval palace or simply holding up a tenement kitchen, a single arch of an aqueduct rising forlorn behind ring-road garages and workshops, a church only spotted because its cupola rises up above an apartment building. Pagan temples sit on intersections, while others are pressed into use as Christian churches; one forms the side of the Rome stock exchange. And 'SPQR' (Senatus PopulusQue Romanus – the Senate and people of Rome), borne on the standards of ancient Rome, famously in the film *Spartacus*, is still carved on every drain cover and city council notice.

At its height ancient Rome had a population of a size – one million inhabitants – which was not reached in cities elsewhere in Europe until many centuries later. From first-century emperors and Renaissance popes, to Napoleon, Garibaldi and Mussolini, Italy has suffered and benefited from the conspicuous demonstration of wealth and power. Above all, the vast resources and patronage of both ancient and Renaissance Rome have all contributed to the superlative architecture and the artistic treasures that lure millions of visitors to the city each year.

A guidebook to Rome seems almost redundant, simply because it is one of the best cities to get lost in. Wandering about is invariably a happy adventure – a much better way of getting to know Rome than by ticking off inventories of worthy monuments – and the city is not large enough for one to go seriously astray. Rome may also be the most written about city in the world. From the first century to the present day it has inspired men and women to try to capture on the written page Rome's fascination and contradictions. These layers of writing and the sense of Rome they build up mirror the history of the city itself.

Yet there is much that can be easily missed. With such a density of history mapped onto its streets I hope in this guidebook to provide some lesser known information about the great sights and to tempt visitors towards some of Rome's many hidden delights. It is impossible to encompass everything this unique city has to offer in a single volume, and different guides have their advantages and their drawbacks. One such guide opts for a Top 10 classification, providing a delightfully certain Top 10 Moments in History (with Romulus and Remus at first place) and Top 10 Classical Roman Writers (Plautus), alongside the more conventional categories of cafés and shops. Others provide a neatness of chronology that disintegrates when applied to the fragmented history on the ground.

Almost all works about Rome are, by necessity, highly selective and probably partisan, and this book is no exception. I regret the churches, palazzi, galleries, views and ruins that space has forced me to exclude, but I have attempted to recreate Rome as it is experienced by anybody discovering it for the first time. So on each walk an early morning market may lead onto a busy modern street, a workman's café or *enoteca* (wine bar) to a fashionable art gallery; a once notorious palazzo emblazoned with battered coats of arms may be tracked down in a tiny piazza; the calm of a quiet cloister may be revealed only seconds from one of Rome's most notorious traffic snarl-ups.

Rome's monuments, though magnificent, are somehow less powerful when viewed in isolation, so as you are guided from street to street, you may shift swiftly from the sublime to the trivial: from a plate of artichokes to a Raphael painting, from a modern magician to Nero's ghost, from the anti-Mafia HQ to second-hand cowboy boots, from Keats to a slow boat up the Tiber. These can be followed on the page and on the street or simply read to gauge the flavour of the different districts and moods of historic Rome.

It is not all perfection of course. Romans can have enough of tourists. Where most waiters, for instance, are friendly and helpful – even though several, particularly older men, cannot speak English – a few are hurried and off-hand and a very few are simply rude. Museums seem to have a policy of employing the uninterested and preoccupied on their ticket desks; taxi drivers can be either passionate advocates and invaluable informants on their city, or monosyllabic and, occasionally, though infrequently, dishonest. Violent crime is uncommon but petty theft can ruin a holiday and has always been a problem in Italy. Recent heavy policing has greatly reduced pickpocketing (well-trained children, mostly gypsies, are often the most adept thieves) but be careful when stopping to gaze at popular sites or on the buses.

Disappointingly, first class music has never really travelled as far south as Rome but the return of opera to the atmospheric setting of the ruined Baths of Caracalla and the free concerts on the Campidoglio are still unforgettable experiences. Churches often host chamber concerts and in the big parks and some of the big piazzas – the Campo de' Fiori for instance and the piazza by St John Lateran – every sort of music is staged, from rock to jazz to symphony orchestras. It is worth going to the excellent information centres to get current programmes (see listings) or buying the magazine *Wanted in Rome*, available at, among other places, the English bookshop in Trastevere and the Anglo-American one down the Via della Vite near the Spanish Steps.

It is much better to eat a street or two away from major tourist attractions (and the restaurants of the luxury hotels). The cafés and restaurants around the Pantheon, the Colosseum and the Piazza Navona, for instance, are expensive, and although the food will be adequate, more authentic dishes and more personal service are available even a little off the beaten track. A good rule is to never enter a restaurant where you are importuned to do so. In all but the obvious tourist restaurants do what the Romans do and simply ask what the waiter or the owner recommends. In cafés, the staple of Roman life, the routine is to pay at the cash desk for what you want and then take the receipt to the bar. It is more expensive to sit at an outdoor table than to sit (or stand) indoors, and while it is true that Romans don't drink cappuccino after breakfast, they are used to tourists who do.

Perhaps the major frustration for visitors to Rome is the frequency and apparent randomness with which major monuments are closed, sometimes for years. (When I first went to Rome with little Italian, I mistook the word *chiusa* – closed – for *chiesa* – church – as the two were so frequently synonymous.) *Per restauro* – for restoration – is usually the excuse. If there is anything you particularly want to see, check beforehand, especially if it is in an out of the way place.

Italy is superficially much less didactic than Britain. Yellow lines are few, parking is random, who dares wins (usually; traffic wardens are slowly beginning to make their presence felt). Traffic, too, is a question of survival of the fittest; it is a brave non-Italian who takes a car onto the streets of Rome, though a hired vespa, together with fantasies from *Roman Holiday*, can be tremendous fun and extend the possibilities of what can be seen. Crossing wide roads can be a challenge. A zebra crossing, often faded almost to obliteration, is not necessarily a safe passage. Make sure drivers can see you and walk firmly forward. The cars do stop. Eye contact helps. Or find a nun and cross beside her! Smoking laws exist in theory but so do smokers in their droves. On the other hand drunkenness is not an Italian vice; the rare drunk you will see or hear will invariably be a non-Italian. What the British regard as sexual harassment, most Italian men regard as a compliment or, at least, *life*, and it is still part of travel on crowded buses or trains and in some dealings with bureaucracy. The Italians do not have a raft of externally enforced regulations but their monolithic public service is entwined in every aspect of daily life. Except for those trying to obtain *permessi* to see specialized sites not normally open to the public, most visitors will never come into contact with this maddening and immoveable part of Roman life, exasperation with which informs the Roman psyche as much as the need to present the *bella figura* (to look good) to the world.

Italy is a committed member of the EEC. Where the British vacillate, fearing further edicts from Brussels and seeing each one as a dilution of national character and sovereignty, the Italians scarcely worry. As one Italian explained, just as the British believe they have to obey European law to the letter, come what may, the Italians take it for granted that they can ignore any element that they dislike. The exiled Italian royal family were forbidden to enter the country until 2002, and then only by surrendering any claims to the throne, yet Mussolini's grand-daughter Alessandra is a serving right-wing politician. There is a weary acceptance of corruption, more a subject for satire than aggressive protest, but feelings about Italy's relationship with the US run high and are reflected in angry graffiti.

*

Sometimes it seems as if all of Rome is just a succession of stage sets, particularly by night. Each piazza, often overlooked by its elaborate church or small palazzo, its fountain in endless cascade, its bright café, its handsome booted policeman, seems to be waiting for the curtain to go up and the chorus to enter. Against the spectacle of their city the Romans act out their lives with flamboyance and terrific style. It is not just Rome but the Romans too who are handsome, sensual and full of persuasive charm even now *la dolce vita* is long gone. The Via Veneto, once the supposed heart of that carefree, hedonistic sweet life which inspired Fellini, is now best known for the strange gallery of withered, mummified monks under the church of S. Maria della Concezione. It is closed at present; they are, apparently, undergoing restoration.

WALK 1

The Campo de' Fiori (including the Ghetto)

- Campo de' Fiori
- Pompey's Theatre
- Via del Pellegrino
- Via Giulia
- Museum of Criminology
- Churches of S. Giovanni dei Fiorentini and S. Maria dell' Orazione é Morte
- Via Gonfalone and Oratory
- Michelangelo's Farnese Arch
- Mascherone Fountain
- Palazzo Farnese
- Palazzo Spada
- S. Barbara dei Librari
- The Ghetto

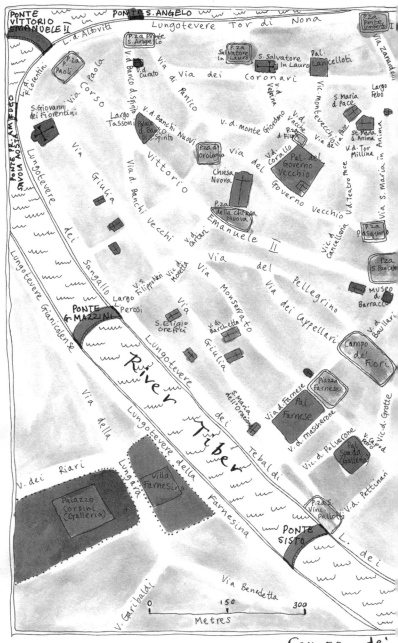

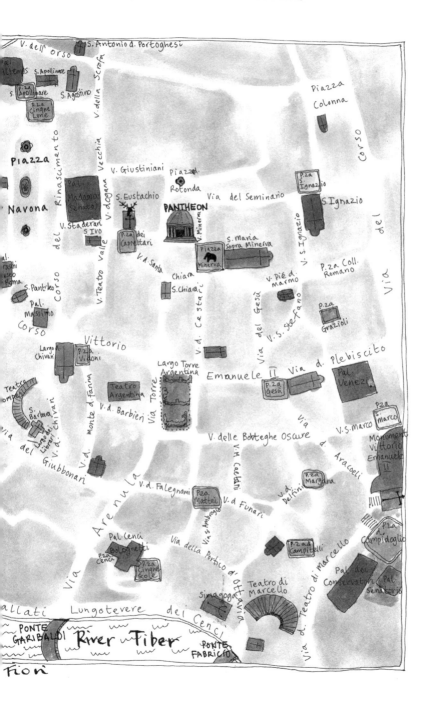

In the area between the Corso Vittorio Emanuele and the Tiber are some of Rome's most appealing streets. This was once the southern part of the ancient Roman **Campus Martius** (Field Of Mars) where soldiers drilled and athletic competitions were held. It is an area dense with history, layer upon layer of it. Ancient remains lie deep in the foundations of many houses, sometimes protruding into the buildings above, and the palazzi of Renaissance princes fade and flake around cool courtyards. Fountains, small piazzas, cobbled alleys and streets that take dog-leg turns around the edge of a church or under an arch; façades that still – just – bear garlands, vines and sixteenth-century dancing girls in fading terracotta paint. There are also notices everywhere, then as now: chiselled stone proscriptions against drunkenness or litter-dropping, statements of ownership, hopes of inter-cession and records of Tiber floods. Most of these are seventeenth-century, but one on **Via Monserrato** marks an official expansion of the symbolic boundary of Rome in the time of the first-century Emperor Claudius. These as much as anything else reveal the lives and concerns of the long-dead citizens of this crowded city. High up on houses and particularly on street corners are *edicole* – or *madonnelle* – shrines and images of the Virgin Mary: sometimes quite simple plaques, at other times large and ornate paintings with cherubs and rosy clouds set in heavy stucco frames. In recent years some of these, previously falling fast into decay, have been restored and dated.

This is an area that is full of people just getting on with their lives despite the tourists and the traffic. Street names indicate the often long-gone trades that once dominated each one: *Barbieri*, the street of the barbers; *Chiaviari*, the street of the locksmiths; *Cappellari*, hatters; *Balestari*, bow-makers; *Pettinari*, comb-makers. The same clustering of trades occurs today, whether of antique shops in Via Monserrato, furniture makers in Cappellari and Pellegrino, small tailors in the streets off Via Giulia or simply the pulsing modern boutiques and cavelike shoe shops in Giubbonari, which echo the street's original trade: *Giubbonari* means clothiers.

Craftsmen still have their workshops – especially in the tiny side streets which smell of wood shavings and turpentine on a warm day – and there is still a market every morning on the **Campo de' Fiori**. Here is a good place to start this walk. The Field of Flowers, despite its pretty name, has a history no more benign than that of the Field of Mars: executions were held here,

Hot chestnuts, Campo de' Fiori

including the burning at the stake of the heretic Giordano Bruno, one of whose crimes was to hold the heterodox belief that the planets moved round the sun. His dark, cowled image looks down on the animated stallholders, pizza-devouring tourists and the occasional prostrate drunk, many of whom take the opportunity to rest on the convenient steps of his statue. The Campo de' Fiori, popular with Romans and visitors alike, has two distinct personalities. By day it is one of the busiest of Rome's markets. Then, in late afternoon, the stalls are removed with surprising speed. For a while the sequin-like fish scales, the crushed carnation heads, the pulped grapes and tomatoes are tired evidence of the morning's work; then the ritual of the street cleaners marks the beginning of the area's second incarnation. The cleaners have bright uniforms and they banter and flirt as they move backwards and forwards with huge brushes to sweep up any market debris into their lorry. The men are young and strong, the women beautiful, their long glossy hair tied back from perfectly made-up faces. Cleaning lorries scour the cobbles with balletic precision, the rotating brushes passing so close to the tables of tourists who are having a late lunch that they stop eating, mouths open, forks poised, ready to take evasive action. No need: the driver knows exactly how close he can come before he spins his machine and whisks clear another corner. On some days the fountain around which the flower stalls cluster is skimmed of its floating petals and drained. Then two cleaners stand inside, scrubbing down the bowl.

No sooner has it begun than it is over. The cleaners buy themselves ice creams, jump into their lorry and go. In late afternoon, the Campo, now a wide empty space, can be at its prettiest and the irregular contours of the surrounding roofs and the soft colours of the façades are seen at their best. In the evening it is simply *the* place to be – especially if you are young.

There is a cinema here, numerous restaurants and some very cool bars. There are street musicians, some truly dire, others almost professional. A jazz trio even has the passers-by stopping to listen. Occasionally there are concerts, where the pulsing of the amplifiers scarcely travels beyond the piazza itself, the sound lost in the twists and turns of the side streets. So many people come here late at night that the overspill from one bar meets the overspill of another in one affable, buzzing mêlée, quite free of the sense of threat that clouds so many north European cities after dark. The young people of Rome do not seem to have a drink problem, though they may well have a *talk* problem: just as in the old rabbinical observation 'Two Jews, three opinions', so also 'Two Romans, three conversations': the one that they are having with each other, and that which each of them is simultaneously having

Street musicians, Campo de' Fiori

Night, Campo de' Fiori area

The Madonna of the Cables, Campo de' Fiori area

on the omnipresent mobile phone. The hum of conversation lasts well into the small hours, and by the time it all closes down the market traders are stirring again.

Start early, coming to the piazza with the Roman housewives to browse among the fruit and vegetables. The few early-morning bars serve espresso to market traders and the day is still cool.

This is a proper food market, not yet diluted by tables of fake designer handbags or cheap CD stalls (although these can all be found in streets off the piazza). It is a particularly good place (though not the cheapest) for fruit and vegetables, and the fresh fish at the end by Piazza Biscione are tempting in the morning's early coolness (though by the end of a hot day they may acquire a more pungent redolence). The ingredients for a picnic can be assembled here, augmented by bread or sweet and savoury pastries from *Forno il Campo*, the excellent traditional – and traditionally crowded – bakers on the corner with Via dei Cappellari and Via di Bauliari, and cold meats from *Antica Norceria Viola* at Campo de' Fiori 43.

On the corner opposite, between Via del Giubbonari and Via Balestari, a traditional local *alimentaria* has its windows blocked floor to ceiling with tins and packets. All packaged Italian food, especially dried pasta and biscuits, bears medals, like the aged heroes of an ancient military campaign. The 1881 Lausanne Gold Medal, First Prize of the 1904 Fair, the Red

Wine shop, Campo de' Fiori

Riband of the Concourse of Turin. Rosetted and sashed, the goods declare themselves winners of unknown contests. The window here displays wines commemorating the dodgier figures of modern history. Mussolini wine, for example, comes either with a label depicting a contemplative Duce or with one that shows him in a more familiar chin-juttingly aggressive stance. Tucked underneath is Hitler wine available either in a full-size bottle or as a set of miniatures whose labels feature six or eight different photographs. Hitler was, of course, teetotal.

Leave the piazza by the north-eastern corner leading straight into the tiny Piazza Biscione, which acts as a pendant to Campo de' Fiori. To one side, covered in ivy, is the tall, shuttered *Campo de' Fiori hotel*. There is simple accommodation in this good if sometimes noisy location, and there is the bonus of a roof terrace that commands a view over the rooftops and cupolas of the area. Opposite, a sixteenth-century house with an old brown exterior still has a painted frieze of leaves and figures. To its right a covered alley, paved and dark, with a small shrine to the Virgin and iron gates which are open by day, leads under the buildings and into the quiet crescent of the **Via di Grotte Pinta**. Immediately to the right is a sooty chantry, now converted to a school of decorative art. Beyond it a tall curved apartment building follows the shape of the narrow street. The buildings follow the wall of the once huge first-century BC **Pompey's Theatre**. This vast architectural complex is where Julius Caesar was assassinated in 44 BC, an act that brought the Roman Republic to an end.

I beg you, if I may without offence, show me where is your dark corner. I have looked for you in the lesser Campus, in the Circus, in all the booksellers' shops, in the hallowed temple of great Jove. And when I was in Pompey's portico, I stopped all the women there, my friend.

Catullus LV

For one of the best and certainly most affable places to lunch in this plexus of alleys, and for a chance to see another – this time subterranean – chunk of Pompey's Theatre, return through the alley and turn right off the Piazza Biscione. The outdoor tables of the restaurant *Grotte de Teatro di Pompeo* are excellently placed for watching Roman life, although in the heat of summer the blast of their internal air-conditioning also has its charms. The rear wall is composed of massive blocks of masonry which once formed part of the ancient theatre and, if they are not too busy, one of the amiable middle-aged waiters may well show you the vaults of the theatre that survive in the cellar. The menu is comprehensive but plenty more dishes are available, depending on the day's haul from the market. (Ordering 'off-menu' and on your waiter's advice is the exception, rather than the rule, in Rome.) The panna cotta with wild strawberries is as good as any in the city, and in late summer two or three mushrooms each the size of a man's hand sit in a basket at the door, or are paraded round the tables with pride. Carved like a joint and cooked with garlic, the *funghi* arrive in sizzling slices, their green and slightly deliquescent centres tasting surprisingly delicate.

Virtually all the buildings in this area have ancient remains in their vaults. The *Hotel Teatro di Pompeo* is a small, comfortable establishment which uses the vaults as its breakfast room, and *Costanza*, a restaurant at Piazza del Paradiso, is another that trades within solid early Roman masonry.

Exploring around the Campo de' Fiori requires a certain amount of weaving backwards and forwards. This is an area of background and atmosphere rather than great monuments; duck under archways, take the narrowest of lanes, get thoroughly lost. You will discover that numberless discoveries await. From the Campo de' Fiori, various streets run from the north-western side of the square but converge before joining Via Monserrato. **Via del Pellegrino, Via dei Cappellari** and **Via Monserrato** are all streets that should be wandered through at leisure. Pellegrino was once the main route for pilgrims, who often stayed in one of the Campo de' Fiori's many inns before walking to St Peter's. It remains medieval in appearance, with charms that are faded by day and shadowy by night; the market carts that lie sheltered in alcoves and side alleys can be no different to those in use hundreds of years ago. As in so much of this area old houses are now divided into often tiny apartments, the occasional chic boutique or jeweller's sits stylishly beside food or hardware shops serving the local population, and fashionable wine bars and hearty trattoria jostle together serving overlapping lives. *Walter*, at number 107, is a trattoria with a tranche of tables set outside along the street wall. It looks nothing special but let the waiters, old hands with a dry humour, judge your appetite, bring you the best dishes of the day and the house red, and you will eat well and relatively cheaply.

Cappellari converges with Pellegrino and then with Monserrato, a street of equal age but historically greater affluence with some fine houses, including the seventeenth-century **Venerable English College**, a training college for priests. There are some good seafood restaurants in the street. For the best oysters, there is *Monserrato* and at a popular Roman restaurant, *Pierluigi*, in tiny Piazza Ricci, queues form by 9.00: the waiters have little time to linger and all because of the chef's way with fish. The street then crosses the eastern end of the rather forlorn **Largo Moretta** – not really a piazza, more an absence of buildings. Mussolini cut a swathe through here, hoping to open up a grand vista to the Tiber. He never made it. Interrupted by war, his plans came to a dead end, never more clearly demonstrated than by the abruptly terminated façade of the once fine baroque church of **S. Filippo Neri** which, having had its broken masonry tidied up, now exists simply as a *memento mori*. The grocery chain *Spar* has a shop here; in Italy it is called *De Spar*, but the tight conjunction of letters reads 'Despair' to any English-speaker taking a cursory look. It is open every day of the week. The logo and colours are blandly pan-European but the chaos, the superfluity of staff, the lethally placed boxes and the more perfunctory style of Roman service are entirely Italian.

Arch of the Farnese Palace

At Largo Moretta, Monserrato becomes Via dei Banchi Vecchi, but to the left the slender curve of the alley, **Vicolo del Malpasso** – Bad-Step Alley – is a reminder that this was once an area of prostitutes, servicing the river trade. Unlike the Appian Way and the area around the Baths of Caracalla where prostitution has continued to loiter since antiquity, Malpasso now leads quietly and respectably into the affluent **Via Giulia**. A *good* step might be to try the robust Sardinian specialities at *Il Drappo* (Vicolo del Malpasso 9). Banchi Vecchi itself is quieter and more sedate than the streets nearer the Campo de' Fiori but under sometimes dramatically beautiful upper façades (this is another street where glancing upwards is as revealing as gazing at what presents itself at eye level), there are a few excellent – and

Mascherone Fountain

slightly eccentric – shops and restaurants. At number 24 an old-fashioned pharmacy occupies the charming **Palazzo dei Pupazzo**, at number 124 a specialist tea shop, *BiblioTea*, serves and sells coffee and chocolate as well as tea and all its accessories, and number 125 is the workshop of sculptor Pietro Simonelli, whose classical and baroque reproductions are packed into the narrow window and can be seen in fragments in rooms white with plaster dust that stretch back from the narrow frontage. At number 129a is *Il Pagliacci*, a very cool, constrained restaurant, all under-stated style, with an exciting – if expensive – menu by a renowned chef, and a wine list to match. This is no place for the casual passer-by, but it is a real delight for the gourmand who wearies of pasta but loves Italian ingredients. Opposite, after-work drinkers at a fashionable wine bar spill on the pavement.

At the very end on the left, as peaceful Banchi Vecchi debouches into the rather characterless Corso Vittorio Emanuele, is a print shop, *Cav. Pacitti*, at number 59. The tiny shop is usually busy. The infinitely courteous owner stocks a broad selection of original works of art, engravings and prints of the city, not just the Piranesi copies and familiar images seen everywhere else. There are some delightful, and surprisingly cheap, reproductions of sixteenth-century woodcuts and early-nineteenth-century cartoons of the Grand Tourists at work, play, self-improvement and self-destruction. The owner is willing to search for depictions of almost any topic or sight connected with Rome; if superior souvenirs or genuine antiques are your thing, this is the shop.

●

It was also the cause of my making acquaintance with certain hunters after curiosities, who followed in the track of those Lombard peasants who used to come to Rome to till the vineyards at the proper season. While digging the ground, they frequently turned up antique medals, agates, chrysoprases, cornelians, and cameos; also sometimes jewels, as, for instance, emeralds, sapphires, diamonds, and rubies. The peasants used to sell things of this sort to the traders for a mere trifle; and I very often, when I met them, paid the latter several times as many golden crowns as they had given giulios for some object. Independently of the profit I made by this traffic, which was at least tenfold, it brought me also into agreeable relations with nearly all the cardinals of Rome. I will only touch upon a few of the most notable and the rarest of these curiosities. There came into my hands, among many other fragments, the head of a dolphin about as big as a good-sized ballot-bean. Not only was the style of this head extremely beautiful, but nature had here far surpassed art; for the stone was an emerald of such good colour, that the man who bought it from me for tens of crowns sold it again for hundreds after setting it as a finger-ring. I will mention another kind of gem; this was a magnificent topaz; and here art equalled nature; it was as large as a big hazel-nut, with the head of Minerva in a style of inconceivable beauty. I remember yet another precious stone, different from these; it was a cameo, engraved with Hercules binding Cerberus of the triple throat; such was its beauty and the skill of its workmanship, that our great Michel Agnolo protested he had never seen anything so wonderful.

Benvenuto Cellini, C16

Turning left at the end of the street and staying on the same side of the Corso, heading towards the river, you will come into the Vicolo dell' Oro. *Taverna Giulia*, unpromisingly near the Corso, serves wonderful Ligurian food in an ancient house and the traffic is soon left behind. Just beyond it is the Piazza dell' Oro, over which a large church looms, somehow forgotten at the end of one of Rome's most quietly fashionable and elegant streets. Ranged along the pediment, stone bishops, their hands raised in blessing, spout tufts of grass, and opportunist pigeons nest in the niches of the baroque façade. **S. Giovanni dei Fiorentini** should have been an aesthetically triumphant building; almost every great architect of his day wanted to design this church for the Florentine community: Raphael's and Michelangelo's plans were rejected, Sansovino, da Sangallo, Maderno and Corsini all contributed to its final appearance, and Borromini did his bit, later being buried within. Perhaps it is the lack of a central vision that disappoints; or simply that a church designed to catch the eye – and prayers – of pilgrims proceeding along what was then the principal route to St Peter's lost its way when it became stranded just off the Corso. The melancholic Borromini finally stabbed himself to death in 1667 but lingered on for a few days before dying – long enough for him to find, not without difficulty, a confessor and absolution. But his suicide still meant that his tomb, next to the altar, is simple, although he had a lasting monument in many of Rome's greatest churches. Unlike many others, this church is usually open, although with less to tempt the visitor than most others of comparable size. It also has an improbable role as the location of Masses held for pet animals.

The Renaissance street of **Via Giulia** stretches away to the right of S. Giovanni. It is much grander, broader and more architecturally considered than the network of lanes that form so much of this area. It can indeed be argued that Via Giulia is one of the most elegant streets in Rome. In the early sixteenth century, Pope Julius II did what Mussolini was to attempt elsewhere over 400 years later: he cut through the medieval streets abutting the Tiber and commissioned a street that would be reasonably homogeneous in design. His intention was to prevent the bottlenecks, thieving and frequent deaths that occurred on the existing narrow approaches to the Vatican. Although the original plan – to have all the buildings designed by Bramante – failed, many noble families built palazzi on a site which at that time ran down to the Tiber. Artists too, many following their patrons, favoured Via Giulia: Sangallo lived here, as did the brilliant but bellicose Benvenuto Cellini, and even Raphael held a plot of land here, although the house (now a very good speciality olive-oil shop, *Apicius*, at Via Giulia 86) was only completed after his death. Via Giulia's most enduring – and endearing – feature is the ivy-festooned arch that crosses from the Palazzo Farnese to the side of the church opposite.

Today Via Giulia is a sedately handsome cobbled street, still replete with history, although much of it lies behind closed doors. A good time to walk down it is in the early evening when the gates to many of the palazzi in private or diplomatic hands are open, revealing frescoes, statuary, fountains, arches – and, of course, gleaming cars.

It has some of the best antique shops in the city, establishments that display a few fine and often colossal pieces invariably unsullied by any price ticket. A four-foot-high sturdy stone Hercules, a gilt and walnut Second Empire *chiffonier*, a marble relief of the Bacchae and a dark ten-by-eight-foot oil of the Forum stand alone in different windows. These are silent, serious shops and are not for casual browsing: they reflect the *gravitas* and impressive interiors of the great houses around them – and the wallets and tastes of those who live in them. There are also a handful of very good restaurants, several galleries of modern art and some excellent fabric shops and jewellers.

The grandness of Via Giulia is immediately lost in the side streets. Older, narrower and, again, bearing names that grew from quite different pasts, they are worth several diversions. **Via Gonfalone**, to the right, takes its name from the flag bearers – *gonfalonieri* – of the medieval guilds. Their lovely oratory in this street is frustratingly often closed. The best way to see the exceptional interior is to come to a concert; chamber music is played in the winter season (up until June). The entrance to the oratory is in **Vicolo Scimmia** (Monkey Lane). Several of the lanes on this side lead to the sadly decaying but still fascinating façades of what was once the riverside, before the 1870 construction of the embankments that saved the city from floods but removed a whole layer of ancient architecture, trades and lifestyles.

Via della Barchetta – Little Boat Street – on the left is a relic of the days when this was a crossing point over the river. At its far end a simple-looking taverna, *Giulio*, outdoor tables set out under a large white awning, provides reliable food and friendly service, a million miles away in mood from both the sophistication of Via Giulia and the bustle of the Campo de' Fiori, despite its relative actual proximity. Ask what the maitresse d' recommends and eat well. *Pasta primaverde* is typical of the simple flavours in which *Giulio* excels: tiny, tender, green vegetables with home-made *orichiette*.

Via Giulia also has its darker side. At number 52, easily identified by the various police vehicles outside and the dark-suited, dark-sunglassed men who walk briskly from cars with shaded windows through the doorway bomb-security screening apparatus, is the **Headquarters of the Anti-Mafia League**. Large, undisguised and busy, this is as much as anything a public demonstration that Italy is confronting its most serious criminal problem with vigour. There has long been a judicial presence in the street. Running along its Tiber side is the **Carcere Nuova** (New Prison). A heavy, blackened stone building with massive iron grilles over its windows, it was designed by Valadier in 1827. It is possible to enter by a side door at Via Gonfalone 29 and visit the **Museum of Criminology**. Inside are instruments of torture and execution, including the relics of gruesome criminal cases from the times of the popes and their guillotine.

Death is not just the concern but the motif of a strange and rather beautiful church on the right, just before the Farnese arch. This is **S. Maria dell' Orazione e Morte**. This was the mother church of a confraternity dedicated to the retrieval and burial of unclaimed corpses. They roamed throughout the city

*Baroque ornament, S. Maria dell'
Orazione e Morte*

looking for the abandoned dead, and the position of the church also permitted the members to sweep the Tiber for the drowned. Eight thousand bodies were stored in vaults beside the river and the bones were used for baroque decoration rather in the manner of the remains at the **Capuchin Cemetery** under S. Maria della Concezione in the Via Veneto. In the eighteenth and nineteenth centuries these were also a celebrated tourist attraction but the building of the embankments destroyed all but one chamber, which is rarely accessible today. The church itself is only open for Mass but has a darkly funereal beauty. Two nuns pray, side by side, at the front. Otherwise all is silence and the light is low. Huge candles by the altar are extinguished. Every doorknob, every crozier tip, the latch of the confessional and each window catch is in the form of a skull. The whole church from the marble inscriptions on the floor to the tip of its cupola is a *memento mori*. That is, except for the illuminated perspex sign which proclaims 'IHS' in a sunburst of bright colours, the wire running away to the electric plug behind the lectern. It is the exterior which celebrates death in a way that is unfamiliar yet fascinating to modern eyes. Realistic skulls, wreathed and triumphant, decorate the façade, a clepsydra or water clock, marking the hours to death, is mounted over the door and to either side two finely engraved marble plaques remind passers-by of their own mortality. To one side a hunched, skeletal, feathered creature unfolds a banner proclaiming *hodie mihi cras tibi* ('Today me, tomorrow you') and on the other a similar figure exults in finding a dying young man in the countryside.

Next door the **Palazzo Falconieri** bears equally sinister fantastic birds. Two stone falcon-headed figures, huge, angry and with the breasts of women, thrust forward watchfully on the façade.

Beyond the church is life and beauty. From **Michelangelo's Arch**, which spans the road, a curtain of ivy falls, almost to the road. Michelangelo planned to

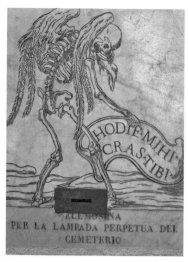

Alms box for the perpetual cemetery lamp, S. Maria dell'Orazione e Morte

link it with the **Farnesina** across the river. This never came to pass and eventually the embankments put paid to any function beyond the considerable pleasure it brings to passers-by. Immediately after it and to the left are the graceful loggias of the rear of the **Palazzo Farnese**, seen at their most striking when illuminated at night. The last eye-catching feature in the Via Giulia is the **Mascherone Fountain**. A grotesque head, over two thousand years old, spews out water (or, on one celebratory occasion, wine) into a deep monumental trough.

Take the Via d. Mascherone to the left. This is a short cobbled street with the high wall of the Farnese Palace to the left and some imposing sixteenth-century houses to the right. Halfway down is the new *Residenze Farnese*, occupying an

Palazzo Falconieri

ex-convent. It is a handsome three-star hotel with the warmth and soul of a country inn, and the position can hardly be bettered. The Italian owners are immensely proud of their new establishment and although the rooms are not in the category of high luxury they are comfortable: a few have a view of the Farnese Palace.

Via d. Mascherone leads into **Piazza Farnese**, a huge open space dominated by the **Palazzo Farnese**, considered to be the finest Renaissance palace in Rome. The two colossal fountains that balance the proportions of the Piazza originated in the Baths of Caracalla **(Walk 10)** and the wide houses to the left as you face the palace are almost aflame with the richness of their rust-coloured exterior. It is arguably one of the most stunning architectural settings in Rome. To the right-hand side the **Church and Convent of S. Brigida**, a Swedish convent, provides some unusual accommodation (the hotel entrance is in Via Monserrato). The nuns, still clothed in the more extreme style of medieval habits, complete with jewelled headbands, run the convent as a hotel, the *Casa di Santa Brigida*. Some attractive antiques furnish simple but spotless rooms, but the bathrooms are a little elderly. It also has a library, a church, the considerable advantage of a roof terrace, and a sublime position. It is, inevitably, a calm and old-fashioned environment – there are no televisions, for instance – but guests of any age or creed may stay here and the faithful, or those who are simply interested, may be allowed to see the first-floor rooms where St Bridget died in 1373.

The **Palazzo Farnese** is not open to the public. It has been in the hands of the French since Napoleonic times and is now the French embassy and the École Française. On some nights the first floor is lit up, revealing to those outside the most richly coloured and magnificent decoration: the ceilings are intricately carved, every surface in the principal rooms is decorated and gilded and the paintings are superb. A sizeable strip of the Piazza Farnese adjacent to the embassy is co-opted as a region of France from time to time. Buckets of sand and bottles of Ricard are imported and suddenly a village *boules* championship is being played in the square, complete with partisan onlookers. On Bastille Day, there is a procession: temperamental grey horses, handsome young officers in breeches and plumed bicornes, a military band, glittering and turning and playing the 'Marseillaise'. Italians look on grinning, half in amusement, half in respect; for those keen on uniforms – and Italians are certainly among those – this is an enviable display.

Away from the Palazzo, in pole position to watch the action, is a corner café, *Caffè Farnese*, under a large and pretty *madonella*.

Return diagonally across Piazza Farnese to leave by the street that runs left as you face the embassy. This takes you immediately into a tiny piazza with a single tree. Immediately beyond it is the enchanting **Palazzo Spada**. The whole front and internal courtyard is covered with ornate stucco mouldings: commentary and figures from Roman history, including Julius Caesar, standing stately and implacable alongside cavorting figures from myth, inscriptions and wreaths and festoons of fruit and flowers. All this is original and typical of Renaissance taste. The Palazzo was once the home of Cardinal Spada but now houses government offices.

However, there is also a small museum displaying the Spada family's collection of paintings, sculpture and antiques in four rich and slightly fading rooms of the period. The hanging of the paintings is old-fashioned but authentic: tiers of them are arranged up the walls, but good information is provided and there are usually few other visitors.

The most famous aspect of the Palazzo Spada can actually be seen without having to pay the rather languid young woman on the ticket desk for entry to the gallery. Step into the first courtyard and through the large windows of a library to the left **Borromini's *trompe l'œil***, his 'perspective', can be seen. This succession of arches, culminating at an antique statue is an illusion. The apparently lengthy arcade is in reality only thirty feet long and the statue is just eighteen inches high. It is much more effective seen from its own courtyard of orange trees, not least when one catches the incredulity and pleasure of other visitors. The gallery entrance is right at the back of the palazzo; walk through the courtyards and turn left. Ask for *il perspettivo* at the entrance desk and you will be directed to it.

A simple family-run restaurant, *Sergio alle Grotte*, can be found squeezed to one side of Vicolo delle Grotte, just beyond the palazzo. Very good for basics, it is relatively cheap. Follow this tatty but not unappealing old street and turn left where it leads into Via del Giubbonari, a seamless amalgam of old and new Rome. There are polychrome window displays of thongs and lace-and-ribbon uplift bras, and there are columns embedded since antiquity. The loud interiors and pierced young assistants in small and fashionable clothes shops alternate with those selling print skirts, white cotton underwear and beige cardigans to an older, local population. On the one hand there is the *alimentaria* on the corner selling a few packets of almost everything to very old Italian ladies and on the other the bars selling coffee, ice cream and pannini to tourists who haven't quite cracked the payment routine. Then there is *Antico Forno Rosscioli*, a hearty delicatessen and enoteca – superb wine with or without beautifully served food: enormous hams, cheeses and salami, and deliciously original puddings. It all comes at a price but by the late evening the atmosphere is mellow and, for the serious wine-lover, it has a list that comforts and excites. Close by, through a wide doorway, there is an old palazzo putting on small-scale operas and a little further on stands the headquarters of the communist party with its small but iconic hammer-and-sickle sign tastefully mounted outside. The HQ is not large but its presence is felt. Smiling and tidily dressed young men hand out flyers and the community noticeboard provides the chance to take music lessons – from, aptly, a Signor Fuga – enter into psychoanalysis, find a room in Via dei Barbieri, give a kitten a home. All Campo de' Fiori life is here. Most useful of all, to anyone with even rudimentary Italian, are the day's newspaper front pages pinned up like an alfresco reading room.

A narrow little piazza, **Largo dei Librari**, lies to the left. Of all the stage-set piazzas in Rome this is perhaps the most charming. It owes its existence to a narrow-fronted baroque church, **S. Barbara dei Librari**, completed in 1676.

A life-size statue of the saint stands over the entrance. Beside her, flames leap upwards from two candelabra while jagged lightning shoots from under her feet. She is the patron saint of sudden death – of miners, artificers, firemen and bombardiers – but specifically among all the others engaged in precarious occupations, this church is dedicated to the book trade. The interior of the church is, despite its small size, as theatrical as the setting might suggest and the connection with books is explicit. *Trompe l'œil* paintwork and polychromatic

Church of S. Barbara dei Librari

marble in the swirling muted colours of endpapers cover every column and ogee. But best of all are the oil paintings of various saints. At first appearance these are the conventional images of any baroque church but these saints have been interrupted in their reading. Books are cast aside by studious monks, volumes dropped in astonishment at angelic visitations. In the floor a marble plaque commends *Sodalibus Bibliopolis*: the brother-hood of the world of books.

Immediately outside S. Barbara a gentle and friendly couple run a small open-fronted shop dispensing ice cream, *spremuta* – a fresh fruit juice – and possibly the best granita in the city. Granita is a mixture of ground ice and puréed fruit: coarser and less sweet than sorbet, it is the perfect restorative on a hot Roman day. Coffee is the traditional flavour in Rome, served with whipped cream, but *mandagorla*, a sort of almond juice, is a speciality of southern Italy: delicate and refreshing with its slightly gritty texture, and like nothing else. Almost next door is the curious evening sight of busy tables of animated people apparently eating fish and chips out of paper. This is, in fact, precisely what they are doing at **Da Filettaro a Santa Barbara**. The battered cod served here is perfect, as are the antipasti that precede it and the house wine that accompanies this robust but simple supper. This is a favourite pitch of a local magician. His tricks are so bad that they are both excruciating and irresistible. He is very popular. See the bendy sword snake round his collar as he pretends to stab himself in the throat to an accompaniment of unconvincing rasps and gurgles, see the glaringly fake cane spout feathery flowers, and the cardboard guillotine descend on his finger – *uno, due, tre* – and finally see the money pour into his upturned toupee.

Turn right out of the Largo and follow Via del Giubbonari back to the Campo de' Fiori or left to come out just south of the Largo di Torre Argentina with its numerous buses, trams and taxis. Or continue with a further walk into the Ghetto.

THE GHETTO

The Ghetto is one of the oldest inhabited parts of Rome. Its fortunes have risen and fallen as have those of the communities living here. Today it is a network of narrow cobbled lanes, invariably cool and shady such is the height of the houses to each side. Immediately outside its boundaries are tiny piazzas where once-powerful families built palazzi that are now faded and half-forgotten, while wall fountains still bring up water from ancient Roman aqueducts. In antiquity this area was central to Roman trade. Along the

Theatre of Marcellus

river the market for oil, meat and particularly fish flourished. The **Theatre of Marcellus** provided entertainment, and ceremonial and formal porticoes were built to receive visiting dignitaries. In the Middle Ages it was a place of unbelievable squalor as oppressive laws crammed the whole Roman Jewish population into a tiny rabbit warren of rooms and houses, exposing them to floods and disease and restricting their occupations to lending money and selling rags.

In the area now known as the Ghetto – larger than the original walled enclosure – the eye is invariably drawn to the next turning or archway, but high above the eye line buttresses, warehouse shutters, ancient roofs and dark iron lanterns are survivals from earlier centuries. Look up to the first floor of some of the large and apparently neglected buildings on the periphery, particularly at night when they are lit inside, to see magnificent painted, beamed and coffered ceilings that date from the sixteenth and seventeenth centuries. Equally, in the oldest houses, near the Tiber, fragments of columns or carvings have become embedded in façades, while in even the simplest apartments hefty Roman marble abuts modern fridges and first-century CE vaults provide subterranean wine cellars for Ghetto houses. Even the water that trickles from the drinking fountains is drawn from an ancient Roman aqueduct.

The personality and mood of the Ghetto has been largely dictated by its proximity to the Tiber, not just through trade but in the recurrent problems of terrible flooding and the benefits of cooling breezes in summer. Substantial clearance of slums – and some rebuilding – was undertaken when the embankments were raised. Today the Ghetto is pleasingly isolated from both the business of the city and from tourism. There are local shops still serving the community and excellent restaurants that preserve the traditions of Romano-Judeo cooking such as *Da Giggetto, Piperno* and *Al Pompiere* which are considered to be among the best in Rome. But the streets are often very quiet and tend to throw up images of Italy that have almost become clichés: the washing hanging across an alley, the clusters of black-dressed grandmothers sitting on hard-backed chairs, boys tinkering with an unpromising motorbike. Yet this has only been a peaceful reality for those who have lived here for the past fifty years of its many centuries.

The Jewish community in Rome is the most ancient in Europe. Originally the Jewish communities lived on both sides of the Tiber with roots in Trastevere as well as here. In 1215 the Papacy demanded that Jews should wear distinctive insignia on their clothing, and they were forced to enter church where they had to listen to sermons which harangued them to convert. In the proscriptions of the Counter-Reformation, a gated wall was built to enclose them within a tiny area between the Portico d'Ottavia and the river, although this was expanded in the early part of the nineteenth century. Little trace remains of these walls today, although a ruined building in **Piazza Costaguti** was part of one gate and another was adjacent to the small church of **S. Gregorio della Divina Pietà**. In time, and particularly after the Italian reunification of 1870, the Jews were fully integrated into Roman society, the Ghetto was abolished, and in 1904 a great synagogue taking its inspiration from Babylonian and Assyrian architecture was built right beside the Tiber. It has its own museum. After Mussolini allied Italy with Germany the situation soon deteriorated.

The rest of the Roman population was largely reluctant to isolate and persecute the Jews in Rome, but in October 1943 German troops entered the Ghetto and 2,091 Jews were deported, mainly to Auschwitz. Only sixteen returned. Several Jews were hidden in homes within the city; indeed, some were even concealed in the warren of rooms within the Theatre of Marcellus. A further 75 Jews were among those shot in the massacre at the Fosse Ardeatine (**Walk 10**).

Start out on **Largo di Torre Argentina**, one of Rome's busier intersections. Traffic hurtles round the square, trams and taxis wait here and pedestrians make desperate attempts to cross. In the centre of this frenetic city scene is an attractive group of ruins, overhung by pine trees and home to numerous cats. These ruins are several feet below today's street level and are not ordinarily accessible, but they are in fact more clearly seen from above. The tower on the corner is twelfth-century but the other remains are of Republican-era temples dating from the third to first centuries BCE, which were discovered during proposed building schemes. The great Theatre of Pompey stretched to this point and tradition has it that Julius Caesar was assassinated on 15 March 44 BCE, at a spot immediately behind the circular temple.

Follow Via Arenula, the street leaving the square to the south, for a short distance and then take the little Via dei Falegnami (Carpenters' Street). Within yards this enters the delightful little **Piazza Mattei**. If there is one reason to walk up here, it is the **Fontana di Tartarughe**, one of Rome's most appealing fountains. Commissioned in the 1580s by the Mattei family, the scrabbling tortoises, which add a touch of wit to the sinuous bronze young men perched on dolphins, were added a century later, possibly by Bernini. (In the early years of the twentieth century a Roman firm created life-size copies of this fountain and they were exported to private owners all over the world. One, bought by a Mr And Mrs W. Crocker, is now on public display in Huntingdon Park, San Francisco.) Once there was a lace shop here, much frequented by nineteenth-century English ladies. Now that the shops are gone there are few passers-by. Sit outside the little bar and watch and listen to the water.

The fine **Palazzo Costaguti** occupies the corner of the piazza on the same side as the bar. Something of its magnificent interior can occasionally be seen by night when the first floor lights are on. It is not open to the public and is rumoured to be in poor condition but it is currently possible to rent a very beautiful apartment inside it by the week (*www.rentalinrome.com/costaguti/costagutiapartment.htm*).

Diagonally opposite this Palazzo, follow the Via dei Funari (Ropemakers Street) as far as the archway to **Palazzo Mattei di Giove**, immediately on the right, on the corner with Via Caetani. The palazzo is home to an American Academy but you can enter the courtyards which are an extraordinarily profuse example of Renaissance display. Busts, statues, reliefs and inscriptions fill every inch of space in an explosion of stone Roman emperors and mythical heroes, and stucco

Via del Portico d'Ottavia

weaponry, laurels and coats of arms. It all continues on the first-floor loggia.

Return to Piazza Mattei and take the Via S. Ambrogio. This is a backstreet alleyway heavy with age and atmosphere where suddenly one feels very far from the city and from the twenty-first century. It curves round to the Via del Portico d'Ottavia, a street running parallel to the river and one of the most important thoroughfares of the area. To one end is the great first-century portico from which it takes its name, but first turn right and walk past the fascinating medieval house, the **Casa di Lorenzo Manili**, covered in inscriptions and fragments of carving that Manili scavenged from the Via Appia (**Walk 10**). Only the head and muscular forelegs of a lion seizing its prey are shown on one broken piece but even so it is full of energy and fine observation. There is even a side of a sarcophagus here with relief busts of an ancient Roman family staring into eternity.

Today we drove through the quarter of the Jews, called the Ghetto degli Ebrai. It is a long street enclosed each end with a strong iron gate, which is locked by the police at a certain hour each evening (I believe it is 10 o' clock) and any Jew found without

Casa di Lorenzo Manilio

its precincts after that time, is liable to punishment
and a heavy fine. The street is narrow and dirty, the
houses wretched and ruinous, and the appearance of
the inhabitants squalid, filthy and miserable – on the
whole it was a painful scene.

Mrs Anna Jameson *Diary of an Ennuyee* (1826)

Scraps of golden fringe; pieces of silk brocade; rags of
velvet; patches of red; scraps of blue and orange,
yellow, black and white. I have never seen the like.
The Jews might patch all creation and make the
whole world as varicoloured as a harlequin.

Ferdinand Gregorovius *History of the
City of Rome in the Middle Ages* (1872)

There were astrologers and diviners and magicians and witches and crystal-gazers among them to whom great ladies came on foot, thickly veiled, and walking delicately amidst the rags, and men too, who were more ashamed of themselves, and slunk in at nightfall to ask the Jews concerning the future – even in our time as in Juvenal's and Juvenal's as in Saul's of old . . . And the diviners and seers and astrologers of the Ghetto were long in high esteem and sometimes earned fortunes when they hit the truth and when the truth was pleasant in the realization.

Francis Marion Crawford *Ave Roma Immortalis* (1928)

The queues at the Jewish bakery in Via del Portico d'Ottavio are a testament to its fame. Try damson or sour cherry and ricotta tart, or almond and honey biscuits, *briscollini* – roasted pumpkin seeds – and *pizza ebraica*, which is not pizza as the rest of Rome knows it but a pastry, rich in raisins, dried fruit, almonds and pine nuts. The space here, now known as the Piazza del Progresso, was once called the Piazza Giudea. A gate near the Portico d'Ottavio sealed the Ghetto and a fountain and a gallows stood on this piazza.

Turn left down the side of the church of S. Maria del Pianto. Ahead lies a large palazzo. This is **Palazzo Cenci**. Turn right then left, left and right to walk all around it. The little street, the Vicolo Monte dei Cenci, rises along the contour of an artificial hill, formed by subterranean ruins, once the Circus Flaminius. Members of the unfortunate Cenci family, especially Beatrice, the daughter of the house, have acquired historical and literary fame through their ghastly end. Beatrice, her brothers and stepmother murdered their brutal, abusing father in 1598 at Petrella in the Sabine hills. They were unsuccessful in covering it up and all were tortured in Rome and then condemned to death by the harsh Pope Clement VIII, except for the youngest brother – who had to watch the executions. Beatrice was beheaded in front of horrified crowds at the end of the Ponte S. Angelo. Shelley, Stendhal, Artaud, Dumas, Swinburne, Moravia, even Alfred Nobel, among many others, retold her tale with enthusiasm and a film was made of her life and death. Modern research suggests that she may not have been quite the seventeen-year-old innocent that the popular version of her story depicts, but she was certainly cruelly mistreated. What is traditionally said to be her portrait by Guido Reni, although it is almost certainly not, nevertheless entranced and inspired Shelley, and hangs in the Palazzo Barberini. The family chapel is near the palazzo but Beatrice's mortal remains lie under the altar of **S. Pietro in Montorio**, Trastevere (**Walk 8**).

The huge complex of Cenci palaces surrounds an ancient and almost enclosed square. The older part is very much as Beatrice would have known it. The very traditional, gently old-fashioned restaurant *Al Pompiere* is on the first floor of the oldest part of the palace. Classic Roman cooking is presented in this room of high-beamed ceilings and frescoes. Outside, an alley, replete with sinister associations but actually just dark, leads off through a low, decaying tunnel, the **Arco dei Cenci**.

●

A manuscript was communicated to me during my travels in Italy, which was copied from the archives of the Cenci Palace at Rome and contains a detailed account of the horrors which ended in the extinction of one of the noblest and richest families of that city, during the Pontificate of Clement VIII, in the year

1599. The story is that an old man, having spent his life in debauchery and wickedness, conceived at length an implacable hatred towards his children; which showed itself towards one daughter under the form of an incestuous passion, aggravated by every circumstance of cruelty and violence. This daughter, after long and vain attempts to escape from what she considered a perpetual contamination both of body and mind, at length plotted with her mother-in-law and brother to murder their common tyrant. The young maiden who was urged to this tremendous deed by an impulse which overpowered its horror was evidently a most gentle and amiable being, a creature formed to adorn and be admired, and thus violently thwarted from her nature by the necessity of circumstance and opinion.

Shelley on Beatrice Cenci, C19

●

Returning to the Via del Portico d'Ottavia, small restaurants line one side, their tables sprawling out right up to the edge of the ruins in summer, their interiors bustling, warm and enclosed in winter. The *Taverna del Ghetto* at Via del Portico d'Ottavia 8 is kosher but all these restaurants serve Jewish food: deep-fried, battered fillet of cod, fried rice and mozzarella balls and tender rosemary-flavoured lamb are just some of the traditional dishes served here, but it is *carciofi alla Giudia* – deep-fried artichokes, oil and salt – that is the famously traditional dish: apparently utterly simple, yet close to perfection in flavour, texture and appearance.

The ruins of the **Portico d'Ottavia** are still imposing but are only a fragment of the original building, erected by the Emperor Augustus and dedicated to his sister Octavia, the long-suffering wife of Mark Anthony. Excavations continue at its base. Within the ruins is a church, **S. Angelo in Pescharia**, the name derived from the large fish market which was held here for centuries. Just beyond the Portico is the massive, battered hulk of the first-century **Theatre of Marcellus**.

In the small space between the various ruins and the end of the road is a plaque fixed to a medieval house. This commemorates the deportation of the Jews of the Ghetto in 1943. A service of commemoration is held here every year. (Over the river on the Trastevere embankment a further inscription, from Lamentations, records the rounding-up of 112 pupils at a school there.)

●

Udite, o genti Guardate il mio dolore
Le mie ragazze ed I miei Giovani sono stati deporti

Hear, oh I pray you, all people, and behold my sorrow
My girls and young men are gone into captivity

Lamentations 1.18

●

This is also the site of one of the gates of the Ghetto. A small church, **S. Giorgio della Divina Pietà**, stood just outside the gates and still stands, permanently closed, between the ruins, the unceasing traffic of the Lungotevere and the Tiber beyond, and the massive synagogue, guarded by armed police since a bomb attack in the 1980s. S. Giorgio's small, forgotten façade bears an admonitory inscription from Isaiah, in Hebrew and Latin: 'All day long I have stretched out my hands to a disobedient and gainsaying people.' This was one of the churches into which the Jews were once forced to listen to Christian sermons.

Cross the Lungotevere and then the small bridge once known as the Jewish Bridge, now known as the **Ponte Fabricio**. It is the oldest functioning bridge over the Tiber (a central span of the older Ponte Rotto still stands downstream, marooned in the current). The pedestrian-only Ponte Fabricio leads to Tiber Island, originally formed by a sandbank in the river and long associated with healing. An unusual four-headed Janus watches over the access to this island, which the ancient Romans said was the ship that had borne the god of healing, Asclepius, to their city some time in the third century BCE. A couple of centuries later, and with pleasing imagination, the story was recollected in the shaping of the tip of the island in stone blocks to resemble a ship. It can still be recognized as such and a carving of Acsclepius can also be seen on the prow. Today there remains a hospital on the spot. The church too is dedicated to **S. Bartholomew**, the patron saint of the sick (and also, perhaps appropriately, of butchers). At mid-morning and mid-afternoon the little coffee bar to the right, just in front of the church, is crowded with white-coated doctors in sunglasses huddling over their espressos and quick cigarettes, or groups of nurses ordering trays of ice cream. The restaurant *Sora Lelle*, next to the medieval tower which once guarded the crossing, is one of Rome's most famous trattoria, offering traditional Roman cooking done with a degree of professional excellence that earns it a place in most guidebooks and a constant – though, in the tourist season, heavily American – clientele.

Continuing along the bridge from the far side of the island brings you straight into Trastevere (**Walk 7**). But for now, return back over the Ponte Fabricio to the Ghetto, back past the Portico d'Ottavia. Immediately to its left-hand side, as you face it, between the columns and the *Restaurant da Giggetto*, a little alley runs under an arch. Take this and bear right. This is a perfect slice of old Rome: marble fragments, odd roof levels, age-old drinking fountains and warehouse doors – and none of it over-restored. It has survived rather than been preserved. Take the next left up a lane. The view of the **Theatre of Marcellus** is good from here: on a summer's evening you can stand in the dim light of this cobbled cul-de-sac and listen to the concerts which take place beside the ancient theatre. In nearly 2,000 years the theatre has been a magnificent place of reception and entertainment on the Tiber, a medieval fortress, and a palazzo with shops clustered in the arches below. It has been in the possession of great men and great families by turns from Augustus to the Pierleone, Savelli and Orsini families. While fortunate residents still live on its upper floors, the ancient arcades were cleared of all accretions in the 1920s and 1930s and it is now strangely remote from the life that swirls around it.

Return to the main street and continue up the Via Tribuna della Campitelli. As it comes into **Piazza Campitelli** the immaculate tables and formally dressed waiters of the restaurant *Vecchia Roma* occupy the corner behind low hedges and under linen umbrellas. The interior of this elegant restaurant is attractive too and the food, wine and prices are what you would expect from one of Rome's more famous institutions. In high season, confident American and English voices tend to drown out all others and the Italian diners are overly attached to their mobiles. But it is unquestionably a pleasant spot and the fish, in particular, is quite excellent.

For a simpler experience in what must be one of the most perfect settings in central Rome go straight ahead, up the Via dei Delfini for a short distance. The **Piazza Margana** is a very quiet, tiny open space with a twelfth-century tower, an old palazzo, ivy-covered houses and a tree. Here is a peace seldom disturbed; even the nice but ubiquitous man with the zither never makes it up here. It has a fairly sophisticated wine bar, *Vivando*, and a rustic-style taverna, the *Taverna degli Amici*. Here the food is best in the basics: good pasta, house wine in earthenware jugs, better than average puddings. The service is competent, if a little reserved, but atmosphere is all. The wine bar, too, tucked away right in a corner, has that feeling of a new enterprise: it is a tiny building, with an uncluttered interior, few customers and service careful and a little slow. Nevertheless, to sit in the back room with low-volume Spanish guitar playing and have a chance to sample some exceptional wine is a pleasantly low-key, relaxing experience. Food is served here too, mostly modern, with some rather challenging flavours and combinations, and a wonderful ham sits on the counter. But it is as a wine bar that *Vivando* comes into its own.

Behind Piazza Margana, take the Via dei Delfini and turn right into Via Caetani. Via Caetani is a reminder that these quaint streets are not a film set for a historical romance. It was here that the body of Aldo Moro, leader of the Christian Democratic party, was found after his kidnap and murder by the Red Brigades in 1978. A plaque marks the spot.

Caetani goes straight into Via delle Botteghe Oscure, a wide and largely unattractive street created by late-nineteenth-century road-widening schemes and leading back to the Largo di Torre Argentina to the left. At Via delle Botteghe Oscure 31, **Crypta Balbi** is one of Rome's newest museums and is an exciting structure in its own right, combining excavated ruins from the 2,000-year-old Theatre of Balbus with soaring glass ceilings, light wood and slender struts of metal that represent the most innovative of Italian architecture. It fills a gap in the record. For centuries classical Rome dominated museums, exhibitions and the agenda for excavation and preservation. Tranches of unloved medieval buildings were destroyed to expose the ancient remains beneath. Crypta Balbi redresses the balance. Here is a history that focuses on the Middle Ages, the artisans, merchants and religious foundations that dominated and controlled the lives of ordinary Romans. The exhibits are beautifully displayed and explained in the airy upstairs space. In theory the visitor can descend to the excavations below. This is not always the case though no one will tell you this when you buy a ticket. The young man on the desk evidently has his game of patience on his computer poised at a crucial moment and shrugs, in that exquisitely indifferent Roman way, when disgruntled patrons return to ask why the excavations are off limits.

Walk back on into Largo di Torre Argentina: the cats, the ruins, the ghosts of assassination and the old theatre where the first performance of Rossini's *Barber of Seville* (then called *Almaviva*) was a disaster. A plot had been hatched by supporters of another composer to destroy Rossini's reputation. Rossini, in a vicuña coat that had apparently offended the audience as much as the opera had, strode off home to bed. Unlike Caesar, who pulled his toga over his head and succumbed to his assailants' knives.

WALK 2

From the Pantheon to the Piazza Navona

- Via Pié di Marmo
- Piazza Minerva
- S. Maria sopra Minerva
- Pantheon
- S. Ignazio
- Ecclesiastical outfitters
- Churches of S. Ivo in Sapienza and S. Eustachio
- Piazza Navona
- S. Maria della Pace and Cloister
- Via dei Coronari
- Palazzo Altemps
- Via dell' Orso
- Torre della Scimmia
- Pasquino
- Palazzo Massimo della Colonna
- Museum of Rome
- Barracco Museum

Although it was not bisected by the **Corso Vittorio Emanuele** until the nineteenth century the northern part of the ancient Campus Martius has developed a very different personality to its southern section around the Campo de' Fiori. Some of Rome's most stunning sights, not just those of antiquity, are to be seen on this walk, although the ancient past is never far out of sight. But buildings of the baroque period, as well as some of the city's very best small shops and countless tiny cafés can be found in former back streets that have become increasingly fashionable. The energetic and witty spirit of the **Piazza Navona**, at its centre, diffuses through the streets around, and although this is an area which both tourists and Italians love it never seems impossibly overcrowded or lacking in style.

Start by walking up the Via del Gesù north from the point the Corso Vittorio Emanuele becomes Via del Plebiscito. Turn right down little Via del Stefano del Cacco and then left into **Via Pié di Marmo**. The eponymous *pié* is a colossal marble foot, probably part of a statue from some long-vanished temple to the Egyptian gods (these statues became popular in Rome after Augustus conquered Egypt). Continue along this street until it opens into **Piazza Minerva** where there is another relic of the east. A charmingly lifelike baby elephant, designed by Bernini in the seventeenth century, bears an Egyptian obelisk that is thousands of years old, and was brought to the city by ancient Roman antique collectors.

The piazza and its church take their name from a temple to the pagan goddess Minerva that formerly stood on this site. The church, **S. Maria sopra Minerva**, is one of the very few examples of Gothic art in the city and is a numinous counterpoint to the hectic dominance of the baroque everywhere else in Rome. It dates from the thirteenth century. On its side plaques mark the height of historic Tiber floods. This is one of the prettiest churches in Rome. Its graceful interior, with its soaring arches and stars scattered on a blue ceiling, is full of artistic treasures and contains several tombs of the famous including those of Catherine of Siena, Pope Leo X and the artist Fra' Angelico. Among the memorials and the sculpture, the frescoes of the Assumption should not be missed. Fra Lippi's exuberant angelic musicians, clutching their tambors, drums, trumpets and triangles, richly dressed in reds and blues and yellows, chequered, striped, scalloped and gathered, accompany the Virgin Mary through the sky, revealed as if a fissure to the heavens had opened up in the church itself.

For those with unlimited money and who seek five-star luxury, the large hotel in the piazza – *Grand Hotel Minerva* – is one of the better choices in Rome, not least for position; most of the other hotels in this category are clustered in the crowded streets around the Spanish Steps.

Leaving the piazza take Via Minerva, to the right with your back to the church. This comes down the side of Rome's great **Pantheon**, an approach that permits a view of the massive brick arches of the substructure. It was denuded of its marble facings long ago but when it was completed in around CE 128, it must have been a breathtaking sight, an appropriate house for the gods, with its marble facings glaringly white in the Roman light and the gilded bronze decoration dazzling in the sun.

Seen from the **Piazza della Rotonda** itself, the Pantheon is still one of the most dignified and handsome of Rome's ancient ruins. Perhaps it is so because it has been continually in use for nearly 2,000 years, first as a pagan temple and subsequently as a Christian church.

Outside, the Piazza della Rotonda is a bright muddle of café tables, umbrellas, *gelaterie*, scooters easing their way down tiny congested side streets, and tired tourists sprawled in the shade under the rim of the large sixteenth-century fountain. On one corner *La Tazza d'Oro* dispenses refreshing granita and their famous bitter black coffee. The composer Mascagni lived in lodgings overlooking the piazza and behind its fading ochre stucco the *Hotel Sole e Pantheon* has welcomed visitors since the fifteenth century. Guests have ranged from the Renaissance writer Ariosto to Simone de Beauvoir and Jean-Paul Sartre. For many visitors this is the heart of Rome. There is scarcely room in the confined space to step back and get any sense of exterior perspective. But the Pantheon is still a stage where scenes are played out that have not changed much in two millennia: flower-sellers, state funerals, private rendezvous, tourists from all over the world, hawkers and sleeping shapes under the portico.

The Pantheon was designed to make an impact but it was not always so confined on its site. Its original surroundings included a great colonnade that, it has recently been suggested, stretched back far beyond the confines of the present piazza, with open views to the mausoleum of Augustus. A fantasy of obliterating the sixteenth-century surroundings to reveal a broad vista unencumbered by history more recent than that of Imperial Rome was conceived by Mussolini in 1925. Among other ambitious plans to reshape the city, he promised to create a visual corridor from the Pantheon to the Piazza Colonna. To do so would have cut a swathe through the largely medieval streets, including three palaces and possibly a church. It did not happen, although elsewhere in Rome other pet projects destroyed similar areas in pursuit of a self-aggrandising notion of antiquity.

The interior of the Pantheon is one of the glories of ancient architecture. The vaulted roof, made of concrete poured into wooden moulds, remained the greatest such roof span until the 1950s. The coffered concrete ceiling may once have been covered in sheet metal but even rendered as it is today it is stunning. Like so much of Hadrianic design its appearance derives from function, in this case a need to lessen the weight of the ceiling. But on stepping into the dark, circular, unencumbered space from the bright light outside, the eye is taken immediately beyond the vault of the ceiling to the *oculus* – the 'eye' – at the summit of the domed roof. The impact of a single shaft of light pouring through the eight-metre circular opening is unsurpassable theatre. Each season creates its own variety of beauty: in summer the shifting rays of sun turn the floor into a marker of time; in autumn a column of mist sometimes forms and rain falls to lie briefly on the marbled floor before evaporating; and, very occasionally, in winter fine flakes of snow circle downwards. The *oculus* provides the only natural light and much of the ventilation for this unique church.

A quite different sort of drama is achieved in **S. Ignazio**, a short distance due east of the Pantheon along Via del Seminario. Where Hadrian's architect relied on stone and light to create impact in the second-century Pantheon, Andrea Pozzo achieved his effect by fantastic *trompe l'œil* ceiling painting in the seventeenth-century S. Ignazio. Almost vertiginous in its illusions, like the Pantheon it instantly carries the observer upwards to the heavens.

Return to the Pantheon and turn back down the side of it. The parallel lengths of street running behind the Pantheon and back round Piazza Minerva are home to a handful of **ecclesiastical outfitters**. In Via Polombella, Via dei Cestari and Via d. Santa Chiara, the general mood and style of the frontage is sombre, but the articles displayed in the windows are rich and rare. *Ditta Annibale Gammarelli* is perhaps the most famous and here are the magnificent vestments of the highest offices of the Roman Catholic Church in ruby red, rich

Sacred art, Via dei Cestari

purple, fine lace and gold brocade. It would be an exceptional young country priest or new seminarian who could not pass by and dream. Even the socks are sold in appropriate jewel-like colours (although it is a Roman urban myth that the shop will only sell these items to Monsignori, cardinals or bishops and even then only on production of an appropriate accreditation) with 'Gammarelli' printed on their sides. They make soutanes and suits for parish priests as well, albeit those with reasonable family or parochial resources: superfine wool for summer, worsted or broadcloth for winter. But the outfitter's most significant item is its smallest and simplest: the white skullcap of the Pope. *Gammarelli*, by appointment to God's representative on Earth.

Gampieri is another tailor to the priesthood and *De Ritis*, in Via dei Cestari, has more on offer for nuns, although here, as elsewhere, the modest pale blue, beige and grey shades, the short pleated dresses of the modernized orders, are eclipsed by the sartorial glory of the male priesthood. Then there is the *Galleria d'Arte Sacra*, with its gilded shrines, shrine-side candelabra, rosaries, inspirational pictures and ex-voto hearts. Among all these glories utility is not forgotten: one window equips the itinerant cleric with a collapsible crozier and a portable communion set in a case. The case is recognizably the sort in which James Bond would hide his more secular explosive gadgetry. It is not all church-outfitting; one of Rome's best shops for children's clothes and toys traditional and modern is *Babe*, at Via Palombella 22, and squeezed between the triumphs of paganism and Christianity is a good middle-grade hotel. Larger than it looks from outside the *Santa Chiara*, in Via d. Santa Chiara, is an appropriately bright and welcoming haven.

Following Via d. Santa Chiara to the left as you face the rear of the Pantheon, it is a few yards to the church of **S. Ivo in Sapienza**, designed by Borromini and embedded in the palazzo of the same name, once the heart of Rome's old university (*sapienza* means wisdom). See it after Mass on Sundays, pristine and white – it is form, not colour which creates the effects here. The shape of the gilded cupola is said to represent a papal mitre. Should you be both spiritually and physically hungry turn down Via Monterone at the end of Via d. Santa Chiara. At number 85 is a unique restaurant. It is not for everybody – although the mainly French-based food is good – but it *is* for those who are driven by religion (bishops eat here) or for keen observers of its more unusual manifestations. *L'Eau Vive* is run by an order of lay Carmelites as a serious commercial enterprise to raise funds for their missionary work. They wear the national costumes of the countries they come from and speak French, but the experience seems very little different from any other restaurant until at 9.30 the sisters gather round a statue of the Virgin to say a prayer and sing a hymn. Occasionally they enact Bible stories in dance.

Almost next door is **S. Eustachio**, the stag that is the saint's emblem mounted on the church and also carved into the stonework of a little fountain in the passageway between S. Eustachio and S. Ivo. In the small Piazza di S. Eustachio is another of Rome's famous coffee bars. The popularity of their *gran caffè* is assisted by its production in circumstances of utmost secrecy. But *Caffè S. Eustachio* has become much more than a café: it is a tourist destination in its own right, probably better known than the church. Tired foreigners queue and perch at the very few tiny tables outside, looking slightly perplexed that so much fame should derive from such a very small cup, one-third filled. More serious coffee drinkers stand inside, two or three deep at the bar.

Cross Via Teatro Valle to the right and pass down the side of **Palazzo Madama**. The fine array of uniforms – different branches of the security services – and men (it is almost all men one sees) in well-cut suits stems from its present-day function as the Italian Senate. Cross over the unattractive and dusty Corso del Rinascimento and carry straight on down the side road.

One of the greatest pleasures and surprises of Rome is the swift change of mood from one street to another, turning a corner from a busy market to an almost silent cobbled alleyway or crossing a broad road of hurtling traffic to climb steps into a small and hidden park. This is perhaps nowhere more so than when you come into the light and breadth of **Piazza Navona**.

Of all Rome's most famous tourist sights, the Piazza Navona is arguably the one that harbours no germ of disappointment. It is, quite simply, beautiful. It appears to be a perfectly conceived space for outstanding sculptures and

Borromini statue, Piazza Navona

architecture which, despite their grandeur and brilliance, convey both wit and affection for their surroundings. By day its terracotta houses are warm in the sun, its churches contrastingly pale and austere; by night it is softly and superbly lit, its shadows and cascades turning it into something almost unreal. Once the level inside the piazza was lower and filled with water from time to time while the wealthy enjoyed cooling carriage rides. In winter Christmas fairs still continue into the darkness under the stars. Nowhere deserves the crowds that visit it more and its size means that even on a summer's day the ambling families have space to walk and watch the street theatre: human statues – a cavalier, an Egyptian mummy or the Empire State Building; a more than usually adept magician; henna tattooists; portrait sketchers; and the ubiquitous peddlers of towels in the colours of Lazio, Roma or Manchester United.

Another of Rome's charms is that things are often not quite what they first seem. The elliptical shape of this light and spacious piazza derives from its original existence in the late first century, when it was a stadium of the paranoid and murderous emperor Domitian. Ruins of that stadium survive under the church of **S. Agnese in Agone** and in some quantity at the far side of buildings at the north of the stadium. Races and gladiatorial fights were all held here. The church itself is supposedly built on the site where the young St Agnes was stripped, forced into a brothel and finally executed under a later emperor, Diocletian. Her tomb is at **S. Agnese Fuori Le Mura (Walk 5)**.

The three seventeenth-century fountains are all watery fantasies: tritons blowing on shells at the southern end of the piazza, a water god attacking a squid to the north, around him dolphins, gambolling cherubs, crabs and fish. The charm is in the detail. The central fountain of the Four Rivers, designed by Bernini, is a masterpiece of engineering as well as art. Here are the personifi- cations of the gods of the rivers Nile (his head veiled to indicate that the river's source was then

Watching street clowns, Piazza Navona

unknown), Ganges, Danube and Plate, and here water tumbles over Bernini's man-made rocks and crevices amid palm trees, rearing horses, tigers and water snakes. Perched on the top of it all is a massive obelisk. Again and again in Rome the grave architects of the greatest churches seem to explode into animism and sensuality once away from their religious commissions. Thrusting upwards is another of Rome's obelisks, this one originally sited on the Circus of Maxentius out on the Appian Way **(Walk 10)**.

Like so many monuments in Rome, those in the Piazza Navona also bear accretions of history and myth. The proximity of Borromini's church of **S. Agnese in Agone** to Bernini's fountain led to the rumour that the shrouded god of the Nile was actually hiding his face rather than see the flaws

Medieval street near Piazza Navona

in the church and that the other figures are caught in various poses of repugnance and shock. The rules which prevent paddling in the pale turquoise water of the basins are strictly enforced, but stand near them and be cooled by the finest spray. Cafés and restaurants around the piazza, of which there are many, are fairly indistinguishable one from another and all serve decent food, but at a price. Navona has a captive and thirsty audience. There are better places to eat in the backstreets to the west.

Taking the small Largo Febo off the north-western end of the piazza, walk straight across the Via S. Maria in Anima and up the side of the *Raphael Hotel.* The Raphael's façade is completely obliterated by a dark fall of ivy. It is one of Rome's best hotels. The rooms are not huge and the corridors and stairway are surprisingly plain, but the position is as good as anywhere, the antiques and relaxed comfort of its public rooms are delightful, and a superb roof terrace where breakfast and evening drinks are served in fine weather is an amenity beyond value. The hotel gained a degree of fame (or notoriety) when the politician Bettino Craxi had his penthouse on the upper floors and the odd bodyguard – in dark glasses, slick suit and bulging armpit – paced outside. Those days are past now and the Raphael is popular with Europeans wanting small-scale charm without generic international luxury.

Restaurant sign

Take the left-hand fork at the rear corner of the hotel. It takes you down a dark and rather atmospheric alley under the buttress of one of two churches which press in tightly to each side. At the end you come out immediately to the left of the lovely church of **S. Maria della Pace**. The pretty curved porch leads into a particularly harmonious baroque interior, although it is one that, having been closed for a decade for restoration, can still only be seen immediately before Mass. It is worth lingering, not least for the famous fresco of Sibyls painted by Raphael in the **Chigi Chapel**. But the real treat, and one of Rome's best secrets, lies through the doorway immediately to the left as you face the portico. Pass through a small vestibule and come into the quiet light of **Bramante's two-storey cloister**, built in 1500, long before the façade of the present church. Motes of dust are caught in the sunlight, pigeons coo and the stone is smooth and tinged dark yellow

The spire of S. Maria in Anima

with age. The lower columns of the cloister are heavier, the upper storey more gracile and the eye is taken upwards to the patch of blue sky above and, from the far side, coloured whorls of the slender spire of **S. Maria dell' Anima** and the heavy cupola of S. Maria della Pace itself can be seen side by side.

Heavily worn stairs on the left lead up to the higher level where, extraordinarily, there is a small and modern cafeteria, *Café d'Art*. The concept of a cafeteria, which has connotations of railway stations and works outings to the British, is quite different in Italy and signifies a rather chic small restaurant. Here you can eat goat's cheese with honey and spinach baguette, a country salad dressed with marvellously nutty oil or a selection of Italian cold meats teamed with a suggested wine, or simply have a cup of coffee. You can do so at one of the small stone seats set along the periphery of the cloister, where the monks once sat looking down into the courtyard, or at the most modern of tables set under the vaulted ceiling. Perhaps the high spot is the Sunday brunch: mimosas (fresh orange juice and *prosecco*), sweet pastries, eggs, cheeses, espresso and an astonishing peace and all so close to Navona. It is a gem and seems virtually unknown, a state of affairs that cannot last long. Beyond the tables is a good-sized bookshop selling art and history books and there are occasional exhibitions and evening concerts in the lower space.

Coming out of the church, the bar to the right, on the ground floor of an old palazzo (its coat of arms a crayfish), is one of Rome's coolest hang-outs. By day this coolness is hidden from view; it is just a place to enjoy good coffee. *Caffè della Pace* is a place to go late at night and drink cocktails served with small bowls of savoury snacks although a seat at the famous tables with the would-be famous drinkers comes at a price. If you are over thirty it is a place to feel very old.

Continue down the street until it comes into **Via del Governo Vecchio**. Over the last few years this has acquired an increasing number of fashionable boutiques. Big names have arrived in this narrow old street, as have some chic modern art galleries. But it still has immense charm: the bookshops, the cafés, various little frontages displaying curios which are somewhere between junk and antiques and some excellent second-hand clothes shops give it its character. Italy has lagged behind other capitals in marketing old clothes but it is catching up fast. Cowboy boots and leather jackets are staples but there are still some real finds in 1960s cocktail dresses (nearly all in small sizes) and retro accessories and in cashmere jumpers (check for moth holes). Some of the boutiques echo the vintage feel but are in fact producing new designs. There are numerous places to eat, mostly small and informal. *Fratelli Paladini* is at Governo Vecchio 28, selling fresh rolls with cheese or vegetables, and in the evening *Da Baffeto* at 114 serves thin-crust pizza, possibly the best and most authentic in Rome, distinguished by quality rather than range of choice or charm of service. The young staff at little *Mimi e Coro* have more time to chat. This little café at Governo Vecchio 73, with its bright-painted wooden chairs and tables, serves excellent and slightly unusual salads. All along the street there are some quite fine façades above the small commercial premises but perhaps the most beautiful is

Café, Piazza del Fico

the house and library of **Peter the Turk**, an immaculately restored, restrained Renaissance house with a long and lyrical Latin inscription along the street walls describing the conception, labour and eventual birth of the house.

To either side small streets wander off into scruffy but pretty alleys all worth exploring just for their atmosphere – ancient stucco, paint fading in what sunlight comes down between high houses, wrought-iron balconies of greenery and washing, sun-bleached shutters. If there is a place that sums up the area it is the *Bar del Fico*, in the **Piazza del Fico**, a tiny piazza to the right off Governo Vecchio and up Via Corallo. The several tables of Bar del Fico are shaded by the huge fig tree that gives it and the piazza its name. Again, it has two personalities: by night – and particularly inside, where there is bright modern art, long banquettes and exciting decoration – it is an increasingly fashionable meeting place; by day, outside, it is something of a cliché of southern Mediterranean life. Patrons appear to have all the time in the world. Pairs of elderly men play backgammon and chess, another spends two hours with his newspaper, his dog asleep under his table. Everyone appears to know everybody else. The handsome owner in a checked shirt chats to a friend leaning against the wide trunk of the fig tree. It is as nice a place to linger over a single coffee or fresh orange juice as anywhere in Rome.

For lunch, the *Antica Taverna* in an old house on **Monte Giordano** has busy trade despite being tucked away on the crooked intersection of three tiny backstreets on a slight hill. Across the way, vegetables are being sold from a single cart, a father and small son carry the frame of a chair, a hefty and aged stone buttress protrudes into the street, smudged with the paint residues of over-ambitious cars. It is a friendly, relaxed place: stay long enough and you may be moved, to avoid the sun, to a chair across the road and the solace of a *grappa*.

If you continue on up Governo Vecchio it eventually takes a dog-leg to the left and becomes the quieter Banchi Nuovi. Tourists peter out but the food is never better. *Miro* at Banchi Nuovi 8 is a surprise. So often in Rome the least promising entrances lead to the very best cooking. Word of mouth makes a flashy exterior redundant. This is how it is at Miro. A long corridor leads to a large barrel-vaulted room that seems much older than the front of the house. It is a shrine to Calabria, the church and the police. Pastel-hued virgins, crucifixes, a map of southern Italy, and numerous photographs of handsomely booted police officers are hung about the otherwise plain room. There seem to be more family and friends – chatting, chopping, serving in the large kitchen – than patrons, and as pairs of businessmen or a young family or a solitary American come in they are greeted by one of a handful of middle-aged women as if they are welcome strangers who have just happened to drop in at a private house. It is friendly, utterly unpretentious and the food is wonderful. Vegetable antipasti include fine strips of courgette in the deepest-coloured flavoured oil, plump flecked and porphyry-coloured beans, grilled artichokes and spiced cabbage. 'Mixed titbits' is a carnivore's alternative: tiny, sweet morsels of lamb, fiery terracotta-coloured slices of sausages, pale and delicate veal, beef on miniature kebab sticks. Swordfish or a plate of fried seafood are tender, cooked by a chef who knows his fish, while spaghetti alla vongole is a local favourite. Choose a Calabrian wine to accompany this simple feast. For a much younger, more sophisticated experience, but one which is equally well achieved, try *Il Bicchiere di Mastai* at number 52. This is modern cooking underpinned by a first-class wine list.

Turn right and ahead is the **Ponte S. Angelo**, a bridge originally constructed in the second century **(Walk 9)**. Before reaching the bridge, turn right again and into **Via dei Coronari**. This attractive street was once a principal route for pilgrims travelling towards the crossing of Ponte S. Angelo and then on to St Peter's. 'Coronari' means rosary-sellers; then, as now, tourists were soon relieved of their money. The houses to each side are largely fifteenth- and sixteenth-century, while the business of today's Via dei Coronari is antiques. A large and more than averagely elaborate *edicola* (shrine) on the corner could have been assembled from items in the shops it now presides over. It combines a painting of Christ, stucco cherubs, rapturous young angels, some sharp-edged rays of sun and an elaborate iron sconce which holds an old-fashioned street lamp. Affluence has ensured that the street is beautifully maintained, but in some ways it lacks the atmosphere and charm of the less self-conscious side streets. Halfway down and just off to the left, the late sixteenth-century church of **S. Salvatore in Lauro** contains an intriguing black Madonna dressed in a brocade gown, and a good-sized cloister. Piazza Lancelotti, also off to the left, is another of this area's timeless spots, much less sophisticated than the tidy Via dei Coronari.

●

Miriam herself came forth, and making her way through some of the intricacies of the city, entered what might be called either a widening of a street, or a small piazza. The neighborhood comprised a baker's oven, emitting the usual fragrance of sour bread; a shoe shop; a linen-draper's shop; a pipe and cigar shop; a lottery office; a station for French soldiers, with a sentinel pacing in front; and a fruit-stand, at which a Roman matron was selling the dried kernels of chestnuts, wretched little figs, and some bouquets of yesterday. A church, of course, was near at hand, the façade of which ascended into lofty pinnacles, whereon were perched two or three winged figures of stone, either angelic or allegorical, blowing stone trumpets in close vicinity to the upper windows of an old and shabby palace.

Nathaniel Hawthorne *The Marble Faun*

Via dei Coronari eventually comes into **Piazza di Tor Sanguigna**. A fairly substantial section of Domitian's stadium was exposed in the 1930s and can be seen on the right. Its archaeological strata provide an interesting marker of the differences in ground level between the first century CE and today. Floods, fires, collapse, silt and simply the deposits of the passage of time have raised the city by many feet. Turning left and immediately right over Via Zanardelli and into Vicolo S. Apollinare, the rather solid building ahead is the **Palazzo Altemps**. One of the frustrations of Rome is the frequency and randomness with which famous buildings or collections close, often for years at a time. Palazzo Altemps is a very positive example of a building that has emerged from its years of restoration, having been bought by the city council, after decades of neglect as a seminary. Not only is this an exceptional Renaissance palazzo but the collection, now part of the **National Museum of Rome**, that has been assembled here has some magnificent pieces sensitively displayed. (It is well worth travelling out beyond Testaccio (**Walk 6**) to Via Ostiense to see the daring and clever display of ancient sculpture at the **Montemartini power station** (part of the Capitoline museums), to appreciate the very different way in which ancient art can be displayed. At Montemartini the works stand among the ceiling-high decommissioned machinery of Rome's first power station, a symbol of public amenity; at Palazzo Altemps they are set in a context of private power and beauty of quite a different kind.)

Built in around 1470 the Palazzo Altemps has a breath-taking interior on two storeys around a courtyard. It is full of light and exquisite details such as a shell grotto, frescoes and ceiling paintings of myths and historical events, animals and birds – from doves to turkeys – a row of imperial busts on the loggia, and a small, dark, richly decorated chapel. It is also gently informative about the process and extent of the structure's architectural restoration. Its treasures include the ancient Greek sculpture known as the **Ludovisi Throne** (in which a dewy and smiling Aphrodite is welcomed from the waves by two nymphs) and one of the most emotionally powerful pieces of statuary anywhere: the **Gaul committing suicide, with his dead wife**, a tableau in which the warrior supports the dead weight of his wife's body while plunging his sword into his own breast. All the pathos of the statue is expressed in the limp fingers of the woman's hand (which may have been restored by Bernini). The museum shops of Rome are undoubtedly the best resource in the city for the seeker after superior souvenirs. This one is no exception.

Walk on up the entrance side of the palazzo and into another nexus of narrow streets, coming into the Via dell' Orso at right angles and turning right. This street, still full of character, was once the location of numerous inns for travellers. One, the **Hostaria dell' Orso**, survives, although no longer as a hotel, but there are a few cafés and restaurants for the more transient visitor. *La Mandragola* at Via dell' Orso 71 is slightly more adventurous than it appears, and its fish is excellent: gilthead cooked with citrus fruits, anchovy and aubergine pie, and typical *cacciuco* – soup made from fish, tomatoes and wine – from Livorno.

●

Flinging aside the morbid hesitation, and the dallyings with his own wishes, which he had permitted to influence his mind throughout the day, he now hastened to the Via Portoghese. Soon the old palace stood before him, with its massive tower rising into the clouded night; obscured from view at its midmost elevation, but revealed again, higher upward, by the Virgin's lamp that twinkled on the summit. Feeble as it was, in the broad, surrounding gloom, that little ray made no inconsiderable illumination among Kenyon's sombre thoughts; for; remembering Miriam's last words, a fantasy had seized him that he should find the sacred lamp extinguished.

And even while he stood gazing, as a mariner at the star in which he put his trust, the light quivered, sank, gleamed up again, and finally went out, leaving the battlements of Hilda's tower in utter darkness. For the first time in centuries, the consecrated and legendary flame before the loftiest shrine in Rome had ceased to burn.

Nathaniel Hawthorne *The Marble Faun*

●

Via dell' Orso turns almost imperceptibly into Via dei Portoghesi. There is something rather Gothic about this short street – not least the medieval tower at its start and the slightly forbidding church of **S. Antonio dei Portoghesi**, the national church of the Portugese community. The tower, rising above a sooty portico, is a remnant of the fortified palazzo of the once-powerful Frangipane family, and is popularly known as the **Torre della Scimmia** (the Monkey Tower). The story goes that in the seventeenth century a pet monkey seized the infant child of the family and ran up the tower with it. The father prayed to the Virgin for the baby's safe return and when the monkey came down with the unharmed infant a statue of Mary was put up at the top of the tower and a light maintained there ever since. There is a long-established old-fashioned hotel here, the *Hotel dei Portoghesi*. It has a lovely position in this cluster of old buildings on what feels like a forgotten street. Rooms have been recently modernized and a flowery terrace has a view of the Torre.

Continue on until the street comes to a T-junction with Via della Scrofa. An outpost – or, more correctly, an in-post –

Torre della Scimmia ('Monkey Tower')

of the famous Trastevere cheese shop and delicatessen, *Volpetti* is at Via della Scrofa 31. It merits a visit as much to indulge the senses of sight and smell as that of taste, although porchetta in fresh bread is irresistible. Turn right down this street and right again to come into Piazza di Cinque Lune and the northern end of Piazza Navona.

Walk down the piazza and cross the street at the bottom. To go left at this point brings you into Piazza Pasquino, a small irregular space full of scooters and good cafés. The battered statue, only just recognizable as a human form, is that of **Maestro**

Pasquino. His origin is probably as part of a group of second-century-sculptures from the stadium but he has long had another, more expressive life. From the sixteenth century until now satirical verses have been posted on his torso. These days cartoons appear too, although much of the protest, invariably political, is still in the traditional verse form. Even for non-Italian speakers, the references to Bush and Blair and Berlusconi are fairly unequivocal. He has a 'sister' speaking statue in Madame Lucrezia, by the Palazzo Venezia **(Walk 4)** and a brother, Marforio, now in the Capitoline museums (also **Walk 4**).

Return to the Piazza Navona, cross the bottom and leave by the Via della Posta Vecchia. The apparently unpromising narrow alleyway leads left into **Piazza Massimo alle Colonne**. It is another site in Rome that carries a weight of anecdotes and history disproportionate to its size. A single column is the only visible survival from the Theatre of Domitian that once stood here, but the real splendour of this irregularly shaped little space lies in another beautifully decorated sixteenth-century palazzo which dwarfs the piazza (the entrance and superb main façade are on Corso Vittorio Emanuele). The frescoes of figures now faded to creams and browns gave this palace the nickname *Palazzo Istoriato* (the Illustrated Palace). On 16 March it is possible to attend a Mass in the palazzo which commemorates the brief raising from the dead of the fourteen-year-old Paolo Massimo by S. Fillipo Neri in 1583.

The family was not a fortunate one and their fate is a reminder of the violence that was just as much a feature of the Renaissance as was the brilliance of its art. In the same period as the miraculous resurrection, the five sons of Lelio Massimo murdered his second wife, Vittoria, the second son poisoned the first one and was beheaded for it, Girolamo Massimo died in a battle against Turks, Alessandro was killed in Paris and Ottavio was murdered by a jealous rival. The family became, more prosaically, responsible for running the Roman postal service under Papal authority.

Return to the pedestrianized main street that leads into the Corso Vittorio Emanuele. A few metres after leaving Piazza Massimo alle Colonne a small hat shop on the left has a wide selection of panama hats for summer and felt ones for winter for both men and women. The proprietor is courteous and patient and the need for a hat becomes ever more obvious the longer you linger. Emerge from this brief slice of old-fashioned service to the busy Corso where the **Museum of Rome** in the hefty Palazzo Braschi, closed for years on end '*in restauro*' has reopened at last, displaying objects connected with everyday life in the city from medieval times to the late nineteenth century. On the far side of the Corso is a more eclectic but in many ways more appealing collection, mostly of antiquities, in the **Museo Barracco**, in the attractive small-scale formality of what is popularly called the **Piccola Farnesina**. Walk straight on beyond the Piccola Farnesina and come into the **Campo de' Fiori**, or go left down the Corso Vittorio Emanuele to reach Largo Argentina's choice of buses, trams and taxis.

WALK 3

Spanish Steps to the Trevi Fountain

- Piazza di Spagna
- The Spanish Steps
- The Keats–Shelley Museum
- The Trinità dei Monti
- Villa Medici
- Borghese Gardens and its obelisk
- The galleries of the Villa Borghese and the National Etruscan Museum
- Piazza del Popolo
- Tridente
- Mausoleum of Augustus
- The Ara Pacis
- The print market
- S. Andrea delle Fratte
- Accademia di S. Luca
- The Trevi Fountain
- Palazzo Colonna and the Waxworks Museum

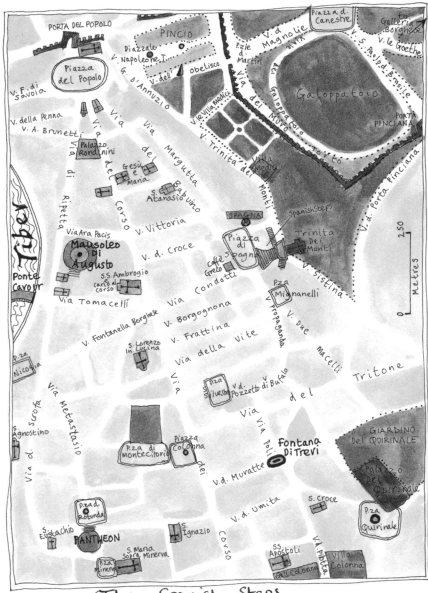

The Spanish Steps

February at the Spanish Steps. A soft, watery sky, the warm colours of the buildings muted, the first buds on the trees and Italians in full possession of their city. Rome in winter is a very different place from its summer incarnation and never more so than here, in the heart of its most popular tourist area.

The **Spanish Steps** were always a focus for foreign visitors. Numerous writers, including George Eliot, Nathaniel Hawthorne, Henry James and William Makepeace Thackeray, recorded the intrigues and challenges of life in nineteenth-century Rome. They all settled in this area to admire the ruins, seek artistic inspiration, buy antiquities – real and fake – and, often, to escape difficulties at home. Roman Catholics, eloping couples, illicit lovers and those in trouble with the law or their families all flocked to Rome. The fashionable season was winter, when disease was less prevalent but the climate still gentle. Members of European royal families, aristocrats with considerable entourages, well-connected young men (and a very few women) with their tutors, wealthy Americans in pursuit of culture, antiquarians in search of a bargain and opportunists on the make. There were English reading rooms, English livery stables, English doctors, English teachers and even an all too obviously English church. A whole industry of artists and dealers in art and antiques followed, all hoping to make money off their rich patrons.

Artists, in inconceivable hats of the middle-ages, and beards (thank Heaven!) of no age at all, flashed picturesque scowls about them from their stations in the throng. One gentleman (connected with the fine arts, I presume) went up and down in a pair of Hessian-boots, with a red beard hanging down on his breast, and his long and bright red hair, plaited into two tails, one on either side of his head, which fell over his shoulders in front of him, very nearly to his waist, and were carefully entwined and braided!

Charles Dickens *Pictures of Italy*

Today the history of the area is still imbued with the ghosts of the grand tourists, and the main business of the place is still making money from visitors – although the designer shops of the Via Condotti and Babuino are as popular with affluent Romans as with foreigners. Many of the city's finest hotels are in these streets, wonderfully comfortable, often set in immaculate gardens, and cocooned against the heat and stridency of central Rome.

Coming out of the Metro at **Spagna** and walking straight ahead, you step straight into the area's mixture of charm and brash commercialism. The **Piazza di Spagna** with its palm trees and horse-drawn carriages is in some ways more like Nice than Italy. From here the great shopping streets of Rome fan away. But to the right are the **Spanish Steps**, still stunning despite the accretions of sightseers and street hawkers, and the ever-attentive police. This wide and graceful connection between the piazza below and the church of **Trinità dei Monti** above was built in 1726; its shallow steps and the ascending curves and baroque decoration are still one of Rome's glories. In May the gaudy beauty of azaleas frames the steps, and at any time the eye is drawn to the very top where the church looks out over Rome. But at the foot of the steps is a delightfully witty fountain, in the shape of a sinking boat, which arrived here well before the steps were in place. The **Fontana della Barcaccia** was commissioned by Pope Urban VIII to commemorate the catastrophic flooding of the Tiber in

1598 and was designed by Pietro and Gian Lorenzo Bernini. In winter its pale blue waters, perpetually in movement, and the intricate details of the carving make the most of its playful charm; in summer it becomes a humidified urban bench for tired tourists.

●

Waters infinitely full of life move along the ancient aqueducts into the great city and dance in the many city squares over white basins of stone and spread out in large, spacious pools and murmur by day and lift up their murmuring to the night, which is vast here and starry and soft with winds. And there are gardens here, unforgettable boulevards, and staircases designed by Michelangelo, staircases constructed on the pattern of downward-gliding waters and, as they descend, widely giving birth to steps out of waves.

Rainer Maria Rilke *Letter* (1903)

●

The three-storey eighteenth-century house (the Casina Rossa) immediately to the right at the foot of the steps contains the **Keats–Shelley Museum.** Keats's cramped rooms are on the second floor and here he died of tuberculosis in February 1821. There is a collection of fascinating and often touching memorabilia of both poets, and a fine collection of first editions. The almost identical rooms above are available for holiday lets through the Landmark Trust. Although never a quiet place even in 1821, today the noise from the crowds below is fairly constant. Visitors to this atmospheric and carefully restored house are more likely to hear the water cannon power-cleaning the steps at dawn than the gently falling water of the fountain.

To the left-hand side of the steps is another English

Babington's tea rooms and Keats–Shelley Museum, Spanish Steps

survival: the famous *Babington's Tea Rooms*, started by the
Misses Babington in 1892 and still selling tea and gentility at
a price. It should be dreadful and full of tourists. It is in fact
rather agreeable. The middle-aged Italian waitresses wear
traditional white aprons and speak good English, the rooms
are cheerful in a nearly English way (polished oak, chintz
curtains) and the selection of teas is vast and interesting.
Snacks are of the high-tea variety and the Scottish scones are
perfect. On a winter's afternoon the guests are all Italian, but
they are Italians *being English*. They talk quietly, their hand
movements are restrained. A middle-aged couple carefully
drink tea from pretty porcelain tea cups. He wears a tweed
jacket, albeit perfectly and rather closely cut, a college tie and
has a signet ring; his chignoned wife is in a bouclé-wool suit

and a fox stole. Two young women in cashmere roll-necks, hair-bands, camel-hair skirts and pashminas are more animated and have acquired a truly Roman quantity of carrier bags from Via Condotti's best shops, but this is an eye-opener for the British. This is what they think we are like. The girls are eating Welsh rarebit.

●

An apartment for a very small family in one of the best situations can seldom be obtained for less than 300 to 500 francs a month. The English almost all prefer to reside in the neighbourhood of the Piazza di Spagna. The best situations are the sunny side of the piazza itself, the Trinità de Monti, the Via Gregoriana and Via Sistina. Less good situations are the Corso, Via Condotti, Via due Macelli, Via Frattina, Capo le Case, Via Felice, Via Quattro Fontane, Via Babuino and Via della Croce in which last, however, are many good apartments. In the last few years many apartments have been prepared for letting in the Via Nazionale and other new streets but the situation is most undesirable except for the families of artists.

Augustus Hare 'Dull-useful information'
from *Walks in Rome* (1872)

●

The climb up the Spanish Steps is a long one. But the climb is rewarded with one of the best views in Rome, city of fine vistas. Turn left as you face the church and walk on. This is a *passeggiata* much loved by Rome's eighteenth- and nineteenth-century visitors. The grand and rather austere house overlooking the city from the Viale Trinità dei Monti is the **Villa Medici**. Built in 1540 it is now the French Academy for Artists and is private property. It holds frequent exhibitions which are open to the public and reveal its beautiful rooms and vaulted corridors. There are also tours of the pretty gardens on most Sundays in summer. Beyond the Villa a flight of steps rises to the **Pincio**.

The Pincio is on the western edge of the extensive **Borghese Gardens**. The view from the belvedere, particularly in the evening, is still the most potent introduction to Rome. Looking west over the haze and the browns, terracottas and golds of a city that seems surprisingly small to bear the weight of so much history it is not necessary to identify specific landmarks, although some, like the huge **Victor Emmanuel Monument**, are so extraordinary that they are unmistakable.

There are cupolas gleaming with bronze, or dull and leaden, all of them inevitably dominated by the great dome of St Peter's. Medieval *campanili*, private roof gardens and the formal architecture of decaying palazzi stand, seemingly without regard to proportion or perspective. Directly across the city is the plateau of the Janiculum, with its trees dark against the sky.

            ●

> The gardens on the Pincio with their fine view of Rome are usually crowded towards evening with both natives and foreigners. The fashionable world appears in carriages with coachmen and footmen in livery, and visits are mutually paid and received. The pedestrians present a lively scene also, varied by the many ecclesiastical costumes . . . perhaps the most noticeable are those of the various seminaries . . . The English and French seminarists wear black gowns; the Scottish violet soutanes with red girdles and black cloaks; the Irish black with red lapels and binding; the Germans and Hungarians (*Collegium Germanicum*), red; the Spanish, black with blue girdles and black capes with blue seams, the Belgians,

Campo de' Fiori

Fontana di Tartarughe, Piazza Costaguti

Trattoria sign, Vicolo delle Grotte, Campo de' Fiori

Oblations for the Lares et Penates (Campo de' Fiori)

Fashionable retro in
Via del Governo
Vecchio

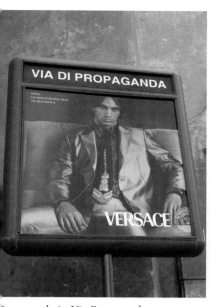

Propaganda in Via Propaganda

Inexplicable legionary, inexplicably at the Spanish Steps

November, Viale Trinità dei Monti

Romulus and Remus

Sacred and profane art, Piazza Mignanelli

black with red seams; the Bohemians, black with yellow and brown striped girdles; Poles, black with green girdles; the Greeks and Ruthenians, blue with red girdles; the North Americans, black with blue lining and red girdles; the South Americans, black with blue girdles and red linings; the Armenians, wide black gowns with red girdles.

Baedeker's *Central Italy and Rome* (1909)

●

The Pincian Hill was never counted within the seven hills of Rome as it lay outside the Ancient City but it was always, even in antiquity, an area of beautiful cultivation. The first that is known of gardens on this spot dates from when they were owned by the general and senator Lucius Licinius Lucullus, who served under the dictator Sulla in the first century BCE. After pursuing a successful political career, he threw his considerable wealth and energy into luxurious living and his name became synonymous with extremes of hedonism. Dictionaries still include 'Lucullan' as an epithet for sumptuousness. Today the whole area of the Borghese Gardens conceals all manner of whimsical delights.

Behind the Pincio, half-hidden in the trees, is an ancient Egyptian obelisk dedicated to Antinous, the favourite of the Emperor Hadrian and who drowned in the Nile in mysterious circumstances. Beyond it there is an almost derelict rustic hunting lodge. Beside it one can hire bicycles, tricycles, children's bikes or covered carriages for pedalling around the gardens' many paths. Nearby is a grotto, a casino, a formal villa serving tea, and a strange water-clock. Everything is slightly neglected, slightly forgotten: ruins of ruins. Rowers move up and down a large lake – boats may be hired here – and on one island a perfect classical temple, its steps covered in resting ducks, emerges from the foliage. The temple is a pastiche of one dedicated to Asclepius; a smaller circular one is named for the goddess Diana and close at hand is a centuries-old copy of the sturdy arch of the African Emperor Lucius Septimius Severus, the military victories of its roundels and inscriptions flaking into time.

Further into the park there is a small canal, a copy of London's Globe theatre which puts on seasonal productions, and a zoo. In summer sunlight it is like walking into a cool house whose corridors, defined by heavy-leafed orange, magnolia and walnut trees, give onto courtyards of gravel, edged with damp flower beds. There are shallow bowls of grass and drier, dustier open spaces where boys kick balls around. Little painted stalls sell sugared sweets, cold drinks and balloons, and rollerskaters skim and leap in the broader spaces of the avenues; the prevailing mood is timeless. Here children feed the ducks, lovers lie close and entangled on grass banks and elderly women take precarious turns on the Viale Madame Letizia. Runners pound up and down the paths, and a woman sometimes passes by talking on her mobile phone while, at the end of its leash, her pristine sheep nibbles at the verges. Fellini would have loved it.

In winter well-wrapped old men talk on benches set into niches in the shrubbery, and small cafés ply a desultory trade. The trails across the gardens are lined with statuary: Italian heroes, patriots, legends, in a display of magnificent moustaches, stern expressions and studied significance. There are soldiers with capes or the quaint hats of Alpine troops, there are men in evening dress and aviators with goggles, but I have only ever found one woman and she, inevitably, is in the garb of a nun. Like emperors, women in the city's history are made invisible by virtue or grotesque by notoriety.

To the far south-east of the park is the famous and newly restored **Borghese Gallery** with its superb collections housed in Cardinal Scipione Borghese's early-seventeenth-century summer house. It is necessary to buy a ticket in advance here, either by personal visit or by telephone booking. It is a treasure house of Italian art. Bernini sculptures, Caravaggio, Raphael and Botticelli are all represented and Canova's infamous statue of a half-naked Princess Paolina Borghese reclines for ever on her cold stone couch. Just beyond the villa is the five-star Aldrovandi Palace Hotel, settled into its gardens and offering well-upholstered comfort and leafy peace at a price. Also at a price (€40 or so for non-residents on weekdays, more at weekends), but one that might seem worth contemplating on a stifling summer's day, is use of the pool and its sun loungers. On the far north-western side of the park the Villa Giulia contains the **National Etruscan Museum**. It is a pretty Renaissance villa with quiet, formal gardens and although its collections are less dramatic than those of the Villa Borghese, it does hold the charming Etruscan sarcophagus of a contented-looking man and his wife dining together.

Return along the southern side of the park and walk down the Viale G. Washington. This makes it possible to come into central Rome from the Piazzale Flaminio through what was once a great ceremonial entrance from the north, the **Porta del Popolo**. This comes into one of Rome's largest and most formal spaces, the **Piazza del Popolo**. The obelisk of Rameses II at its centre was brought to Rome by the Emperor Augustus to mark his conquest of Egypt. It originally stood in the Circus Maximus but was set in its current position in the sixteenth century.

Rome's piazzas are one of its distinctive and very appealing features. Most are small and irregular but some are large and formally laid out. There may be an optimum size for a piazza. The broad Piazza Farnese (**Walk 1**) seems to work well, but Piazza del Popolo is, despite the careful aesthetics of its design, a gusty, somehow unfocused place, where the warmth

Piazza del Popolo

of humanity which is so distinctive of Rome seems to be overwhelmed by both architecture and empty space. Perhaps it is its rather grim associations. Notoriously, and right up until the late nineteenth century, Piazza del Popolo was a place of public execution. The wicked Count Guido Franceschini, whose history Robert Browning retold in *The Ring and the Book*, was beheaded on this spot. It was also the fabled location for Nero's restless ghost, loitering near his alleged grave (under Santa Maria del Popolo, between Piazza del Popolo and Piazzale Flaminio). Nevertheless the cafés at its edge are lively and have a certain colourful sophistication, and of the three churches here S. Maria del Popolo has two superb – and disturbing – Caravaggios. For those in pursuit of less elevated pleasure, a gentleman finding himself in Rome without a hat can take his pick of the elegant if pricey selection at *Borsalino*, Piazza del Popolo 20. Three streets radiate out from the southern end of Piazza del Popolo, and together are known as **Tridente**. Via di Ripetta is to the right, Via del Corso at the centre and Via del Babuino to the left as you face the churches of S. Maria dei Miracoli and S. Maria di Montesanto. All three thoroughfares have changed their characters since the decades of their prime in the eighteenth and nineteenth centuries. However, they also represent different strands in Rome's character.

Via di Ripetta, going south-west, is a reminder that the concerns of Rome, and indeed its man-made beauty, have invariably evolved round the manifestation of power. In this the twentieth century differed little from the first. In Via di Ripetta Augustus and Mussolini's ambitions are delineated in stone. En route to their monuments, the little restaurant *Buca di Ripetta* at Via di Ripetta 36 has imaginative Roman food. The battered tumulus that is the once awe-inspiring **mausoleum of the Emperor Augustus** is currently undergoing a major restoration. It has, in the two thousand years since the emperor's death, been a fortress, a walled garden, a bullfighting arena, an opera hall and a circus. Around it are the disciplined Fascist buildings of the 1930s. This is not the only place in Rome where inscriptions glorifying Mussolini, once censored with a daub of cement, are becoming visible again with the assistance of poor mortar and the elements. Overall, Mussolini bestowed mixed blessings on the architectural heritage of Rome, but he was responsible for the ambitious reassembly of Augustus's magnificent **Ara Pacis**, the Altar of Peace, on the Lungotevere di Augusta, into which Via di Ripetta runs, from fragments found during over 400 years of building works on the Via Lucina.

The building that contains the altar is an austere hangar, but the construction itself is marvellous, not just in its formidable grandeur of symmetry and pristine marble but in the force of its powerful propaganda, depicting the imperial family – numerous, handsome and healthy – in procession. But the altar is most appealing in its human touches. The small children tug on togas for attention or raise their arms to be picked up and right at the bottom, on the river side of the monument, a viper chases chicks from the family nest. As the sculptor suggests, all was not quite the picture of solidarity and dignity that Augustus wished to display to the Roman people; in reality he had no male blood heirs, only a daughter, Julia (banished for her sexual promiscuity).

> Yes, she has poisoned my grandfather and, no, she had not poisoned my father in spite of Tiberius's suspicions – it was a natural gangrene; and yes, she has poisoned Augustus by smearing poison on figs while they were still on the tree; and yes, she has poisoned Agrippa and Lucius as well as Marcellus and Gaius, and yes, she had intercepted my letters to Germanicus, but no, she had not poisoned him – Plancina had done that on her own initiative.

> Robert Graves *I, Claudius*

Turn left into Via Tomacelli, cross the road and after a short distance turn sharp left alongside the Palazzo Borghese (which is closed to the public) along the Monte d'Oro, into the **Largo Fontanella Borghese** to find the outdoor print market. There are probably few bargains to be had, but purchase is not the (sole) pleasure to be had here: the market has all the delights of a museum of images of Rome but with the bonus of being able to rifle through the stands of old photographs, prints and maps. Continue along to the left, across Largo C. Goldoni and into the **Via Condotti**, the beating heart of Rome's most sophisticated shopping area. At number 86, freighted with history and retaining a darkly evocative interior, is *Caffè Greco*. Tennyson lived opposite for a while, as did Thackeray. It was mostly European writers, artists and musicians who met here; their busts, and occasionally their works, are still hanging on the walls in the little rooms of this deep narrow space. It could be worth the expense – history always comes dear in Rome – were it not for the offhand and impatient waiters. It seems that they have had several thousand visitors too many since their golden age in the nineteenth century.

Via Condotti crosses Via del Corso, the central street of Tridente. **The Corso** was once one of Rome's finest streets and the location for the spring carnival and its notoriously rowdy races. Today, the sheer volume of traffic and the weary groups of puzzled tourists and tired shoppers that sprawl along its pavements have all but defeated its historic charisma, while it remains a principal route from north to south across the city. At Via del Corso 18 is the **Casa di Goethe** – the lodgings where Goethe stayed in the 1780s and wrote one of the most famous books about Italy, *The Italian Journey*. His infant (and only) son, Julius, is buried in the Protestant cemetery. Unlike the Keats–Shelley house the interior has not been frozen in time but is a light modern space containing a museum of Goethe's life and works.

Via del Babuino, the most easterly street running out of Piazza del Popolo, once a street of artists and the unconventional, is today an expensive, cosmopolitan thoroughfare. At the Piazza del Popolo end is the luxurious *Hotel de Russie*, much favoured by wealthy foreigners and film stars, and thus by paparazzi. Along the street are exclusive shops off-puttingly empty of customers. Brooches radiate fire from velvet cushions, perfect plump stone boys are poised, arrow in hand, while tiny dark oil paintings of the Roman Campagna are overwhelmed by their gilt frames.

Gargoyle, Via Margutta

A turn left and then right brings you into the quiet and pretty **Via Margutta**, which still carries the resonances of its zenith when the studios of eighteenth- and nineteenth-century artists drew the more affluent visitors – and the more successful models – to their doors. Some of the houses are still studios and there is a faintly bohemian, if prosperous, backstreet mood in the colours, the creepers and the statues. Courtyards, half-seen through arches and open gates, are littered with intriguing architectural and sculptural fragments, and a small wall-fountain with sculptures of malevolent old men is still spouting water crossly. Frederico Fellini, the film director, lived at number 110 until his death. There is nothing bohemian about the chic *Art Hotel* or its black-clad male staff, indistinguishable from priests at first glance. This small hotel with its pretty courtyard is a pleasant alternative to its more opulent sisters in this area, if just as sleek in its immensely fashionable way. The arched windows and, more surprisingly, the altar of the chapel it once was have been incorporated into its quirkily stylish interior.

The end of Via Margutta comes back into Via del Babuino, which swiftly runs into the Piazza di Spagna. This time walk on past the Spanish Steps and onwards to a piazza dominated below by the strident comings and goings at the large American Express office and above by a pagan obelisk surmounted by a bronze crowned Madonna, the **Column of the Immaculate Conception**. On the relevant feast day, 8 December, Roman firemen lay flowers at her feet. After the piazza, take the right-hand fork of the road down Via Propaganda Fide.

On its corner with Via della Vite to the right is a remarkable *gelateria*. It is remarkable not so much for its ice cream but for its ice-cream art. In the windows are explosive displays of titanic cornets. Inside is more and more of the same: *gelati* in wafers and tubs and cones, adorned with whipped cream and fruit and chopped nuts and cascades of silver foil, paper parasols, and even blossom, climb in mountains to a ceiling softly painted with clouds in a cerulean sky. There are no bluebirds singing nor heavenly choirs, but they are there in spirit. Tourists

Colonna del Immacolata, Piazza Mignanelli

peer over every *coupe* and *bombe*. A copper ice-cream-cone dispenser gleams but its potential is overshadowed by what can be wrought not so simply by the hand of man. Uncountable flavours and colours of ice cream and sorbet stretch away along the counter, flavours old and new, sweetly comforting or challenging. The combinations are probably infinite. Certainly perplexing. A short young bearded priest walks animatedly up and down the display. Local office workers pour in on their breaks. There are ice-cream insects, ice-cream spectaculars. Today's speciality would seem to be the *Coupe Roma Antica* (Ancient Rome Cup). This combines the assorted flavours of ice cream with pineapple, kiwi fruit, mango and peach, the whole pierced with a gold swizzle-stick.

Gelateria, Via della Vite

This hardly compares in luxuriousness with a single tremendously large dish which Vitellius dedicated to the Goddess Minerva and named 'Shield of Minerva, the Protectress of the City'. The recipe called for pike livers, pheasant brains, peacock brains, flamingo tongues, and lamprey milts; and the ingredients, collected in every corner of the Empire all the way from the Parthian frontier to the Spanish Straits, were brought to Rome by the naval captains and their triremes.

Suetonius *The Twelve Caesars*

Follow the Via Propaganda into **Via S. Andrea delle Fratte**, with the church on the left. Both Bernini and Borromini contributed work to S. Andrea and the cupola is ornamented with buffalo heads in recognition of the powerful del Bufalo family. Nevertheless, it is the discovery of another cloister, this one from the eighteenth century, which is the real delight. The cloisters of Rome are one of its less vaunted treasures. These peaceful courtyards, which once brought seclusion from the squalor and temptations of the city, still offer a few moments of respite and calm from the traffic and commerce. Walking on, the road forks and although the walk takes the left-hand fork up Via di Nazareno, it is worth peering down the little Via Bufalo to the right. Here more buffalo heads can be seen, carved in relief over the door of an old palazzo. Although near the centre of this busy part of the city, and near all the major sights of the area, the fifty-room luxury *Hotel dei Borgognoni* at Via Bufalo is a surprisingly quiet retreat in a graceful seventeenth-century town house with an inner courtyard and some rooms with private patios.

But if you continue along Via di Nazareno for a minute it

Coat of arms, Via Bufalo

then reaches an intersection of four roads. Crossing over Via del Tritone, which runs approximately left to right, take Via di Stamperia diagonally to the right. The rather splendid Palazzo Carpegna, which stands abreast of the Via di Stamperia and the lane to the left, Vicolo Scavolino, is the **Accademia di S. Luca**. A spiralled ramp designed by Borromini replaces the expected staircase. This academy of arts, founded in the fifteenth century, had members – practising artists and connoisseurs of art – who donated their own works. The eclecticism of the collection only adds to its charm, although it includes works by Titian, Rubens, Guercino and Raphael, Anjelica Kauffman and the resourceful survivor of revolution, Elisabeth Vigee-LeBrun. The gallery is never overwhelming, has some delightful self-portraits, and some of its paintings are pleasingly unfamiliar.

Very near here, off to the left as you face the Accademia, is a restaurant that Italians know to be one of the best in Rome.

It has thus far avoided attracting the hordes of affluent north Europeans and Americans which has been the fate of so many other top-ranking Roman restaurants. *Al Presidente* at Via in Arcione, 95, is minutes from the Trevi fountain and right at the foot of the great walls of the Presidential palace. In this position it ought to be a tourist trattoria, crammed and noisy with overworked waiters dishing out boring staples. Instead it is lovers of good food, plus a few politicians, who come here to enjoy a menu in which fish and game feature strongly but imaginatively, and familiar Roman ingredients are adventurously handled. Dishes such as fried rabbit or lamb with white sauce, capers and rosemary, combine the tastes of the countryside with urban flair. Red mullet is accompanied by asparagus and tagliolini, a pretty *millefeuille* of fish is served with perfectly cooked vegetables, and the subtle flavours of the risotto with meat sauce must be the best in Rome. This is a restaurant run by professionals. Service is friendly yet unobtrusive, gently enthusiastic advice is available but is not forced on you, and the wine list is first-class. It is, inevitably, not cheap, but it is a very good experience. Order the *menu degustazione* for a taste of Rome at its very best.

Beyond the Accademia to the right is the Piazza **Fontana di Trevi**. It is curious that one of the world's most famous tourist destinations should be a fountain. By night and day they come. If it is not the blood and violence of gladiators and fantasies of Christians torn apart by lions in the Colosseum, it is foaming waters gushing over a rock grotto full of stone creatures. The great fountain, built to decorate the back wall of a nobleman's palace, is a superb piece of visual drama, roaring up in a frothing explosion of rocks, horses and spray. By night translucent, palest-blue waters and the craggy shadows are lit to perfection. It is high-baroque creativity at its most unrestrained. It would be wonderful if there were any way of getting a proper perspective on it – but then, the cramped

Fontana di Trevi

surroundings increase the impact. If Piazza del Popolo is too large for coherence, then Piazza Fontana di Trevi is too small.

It is certainly Rome's most popular sight, though probably more for its iconic status in twentieth-century films than as an outstanding example of eighteenth-century design. In high season the whole piazza is a living mass of movement and colour, of cameras snapping, of bemused sightseers, of snacks and sunshades, anxious tour leaders and opportunistic *trattorie* selling indifferent food.

The modern romantic fancy of throwing coins into the fountain to ensure a return to Rome is so persistent that over a thousand euros are retrieved from the waters daily (they go to charity). Originally it was drinking the waters that fulfilled the legend but today (when the waters are probably purer than they have ever been) it is seen as more expedient to give than to take. Mostly the coins are thrown in because other coins have been thrown in; throwing, not returning, has become the point.

If you follow the Via di Lucchesi southwards, the noise and activity of the Trevi area soon dies away. The little streets here are largely residential and a few minutes' detour swiftly brings you into quiet and narrow lanes and forgotten piazzas, where day-to-day life continues away from the fray. *Piccolo Arancio* in Vicolo Scanderberg is deservedly quite well known for serving pizza and pasta with an enthusiasm and at a price which are both surprising, given its proximity to the Trevi fountain. Only minutes from the fountain an immaculate little three-star hotel, predictably called the *Hotel Trevi*, is peacefully tucked up the Vicolo del Babuccio. Again to the left, the Via del Lavatore is worth exploring, not least for its little market which, used by Romans rather than tourists, has retained its sense of untidy authenticity.

●

Late at night the Via del Lavatore is a dead street. The market stalls have been tidied away, and the shutters in front of the little eating places, grey or green with age, blind the façades of the buildings, the way grey or green cataracts blind the aged eye. In the little dead-end side streets are the simple wine shops of the people of the area who live in high-ceilinged rooms in many-storyed tenements. They sit on benches and stools at plain uncovered tables stained by leftovers and spilled wine, and order their half-litre of red or half-litre of white, *dolce* or *secco*.

Wolfgang Koeppen *Death in Rome* (1954)

●

The Via di Lucchesi continues on across the wide Piazza di Pilotta, a place that seems to have lost its way, and under the series of formal arches that span the street ahead. The contents of the gallery in the large **Palazzo Colonna** to the left at Via della Pilotta 17 are in danger of being overwhelmed by a wonderfully rich baroque interior which alone more than justifies the entrance fee. Round the corner, in another, completely separate section of the vast Palazzo is another display, less elevated in tone but just as instructive, albeit not by intent. This is the **Museo delle Cere**, the waxworks, with an entrance in Piazza Apostoli.

If waxworks are supposed to be art, these fail; if they are supposed to illustrate a history of Rome then they are perverse in the extreme. If they are a selective view of Roman culture then they are worrying. The rooms are shabby and the exhibits need straightening and dusting. Waxworks are always slightly creepy but in these few muffled, heavily curtained drawing rooms there is also a strong sense of recently deceased shabby gentility.

The first room is a representation of Mussolini's 1943 cabinet. It is displayed with confidence, the high point of the collection. A faint stirring of national pride reminds the British viewer that the models at Madame Tussaud's have real wigs. The Rome waxworks have seamless wax hair at one with wax heads which are over-large for their bodies – bodies that sit and stand stiffly, slightly askew. They bring to mind nothing so much as the heroes from *Thunderbirds*. The sculptor was not very good at hands (he was not very good at faces either if convincing likenesses are what is required) and most of the models have their fists clenched, which gives even the nicest of them a truculent air. The heat outside hasn't helped; a couple of extremities appear to be melting.

Labels are important where more conventional recognition is impossible. Here are Churchill, Stalin and Roosevelt neatly recorded in one dusty group, while Mona Lisa and Leonardo da Vinci reside in the company of Balzac and Wagner. Poor Khrushchev has a plate cut into the back of his bald skull and

Isabella of Spain has a terrible squint. Lucrezia Borgia's malign reputation is diluted by her adoption of a dress straight from the *Little House on the Prairie* and Josephine attends her strangely tall, dark and handsome Napoleon in a 1970s nylon-lace wedding gown. But it is the Sleeping Beauty whose reclining figure is truly disturbing. Inspired by the famous Beauty of Marylebone Road, she simulates breathing. Her chest rises and falls. But there is something grotesque about her proportions. Here is her head on its faded silken pillow, then there is an anatomical grey area, covered with loose fabric, then, much too far away, the rest of her body continues. The furtive activity under the chest cloth becomes suddenly sinister.

The captains of Lazio and Roma, the two great football teams of Rome, stand next to each other, small, trim and be-blazered with all too evidently interchangeable heads. Next to them are the pop group Pooh!, a band presumably big in Italy a while ago. A *long* while ago. There are, apart from these, no representatives of modern history; time seems to have stood still at the moment of the museum's founding in the 1950s. Unfolding naturally in this sequence is a group of dinosaurs, named as matter-of-factly as Hitler, Lincoln and Dante. No irony seems to be intended. Beside them a leaning figure in red acetate is a Spanish Inquisition torturer and next to him, by grim association, stand the show's most macabre exhibits: an electric chair, a garotting post and a gas chamber. On each instrument a long explanation of the method used to execute victims is displayed. Each ends, with relish and in huge capital letters, with the precise process that induces death. !CARBONIZZATO! concludes the card on the electric chair.

This is not for children – they would be bored to tears. But there is something wonderfully amateur about the Museo delle Cere and it succeeds in taking the visitor back in time, if only to the early years of the last century when a less sophisticated audience might have marvelled at the history revealed in the gloom. It is in its failures that the Museo delle Cere really comes into its own.

Outside, the glare of light, the tide of noise, the extraordinary beauty and skill of ancient and Renaissance sculpture are waiting. Turn right at the end of the street and Piazza Venezia lies ahead.

WALK 4

The Ancient Heart
of the City

- Piazza Venezia
- Victor Emmanuel II Monument
- Church of S. Maria in Aracoeli
- Campidoglio
- Capitoline Museums
- Mamertine Prison
- Trajan's Markets and Column
- The Roman Forum
- The Colosseum
- Nero's Golden House

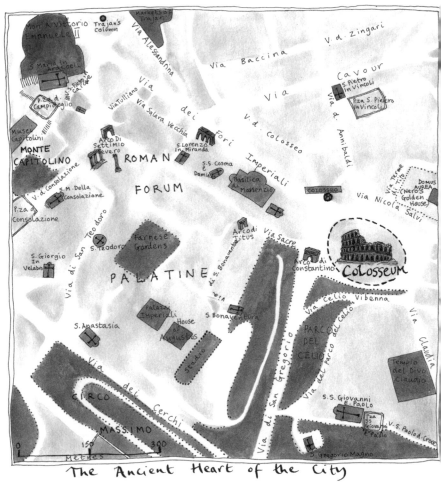

The Ancient Heart of the City

The ruins of ancient Rome are everywhere, scattered in two-thousand-year-old fragments all over its vast empire. Their engineering was so skilled that the Romans' works endured longer than their civilization or their language, while their artistry was such that we still see it as exemplary.

●

> It was at Rome, on the fifteenth of October 1764, as I sat musing amid the ruins of the Capitol, while the barefooted friars were singing vespers in the temple of Jupiter, that the idea of writing the decline and fall of the city first started to my mind.

> Edward Gibbon *Decline and Fall of the Roman Empire*

●

In Rome one of the most attractive aspects of the modern city is that these relics turn up everywhere. The skeletons of many Roman buildings are often much older than the 'flesh' of their façades. Nevertheless, because ancient Rome held a particular power of fascination over the generations that followed, its preservation has, for a long time, been privileged over subsequent building. Much of the medieval fabric has been allowed to fall into decay or has simply been removed in order to expose the older ruins. Mussolini in particular removed whole swathes of medieval building to emphasize the Fascists' self-proclaimed association with antiquity and, in particular, his personal identification with the Emperor Augustus.

But others too have invested time and money to bring ancient Rome to the surface. In particular, the extent of the present-day Forum is quite different from what it was in the days when the Grand Tourists dutifully marvelled at it. Animals were pastured in what was essentially a field, in which the tops of arches and columns were regarded as little more than rocks or shelter for shepherds.

●

That's what is was really like: white marble and more white marble, gilt statues and gilter and giltest. Here's to the memory of the Goths and Vandals – and everyone who lent a wicked hand – the barons who smashed and the popes who pinched and above all the man who found that you can make lime out of marble. God bless them all for the wonderful things they've undone. Rome's much nicer as it is.

Louis MacNeice *Pictures of Rome* (1947)

●

The Forum was not restored to its current state until the nineteenth century. Even those buildings that had survived on the surface of Rome were tidied up in new reverence for the past. The pristine buildings that now stand in isolated splendour – the Theatre of Marcellus is a good example – were cleared of all their subsequent lower-storey accretions of workshops, stores and houses.

The hurtling traffic of the Via dei Fori Imperiali was created by the clearance of a whole quarter of narrow streets in the 1930s. On Mussolini's broad new roads (the Via dei Fori Imperiali was originally designated Via del Imperatore) soldiers could march, parades be held and Roman men exercise their inalienable right to drive fast in their cars. At the end, defining Rome, stood the hulk of the Colosseum.

●

To see it crumbling there, an inch a year; its walls and arches overgrown with green, its corridor open to the day; the long grass growing in its porches; young trees of yesterday springing up on its ragged parapets, and bearing fruit:— to see its pit of fight filled up with earth, and the peaceful cross planted in the centre; to climb into its upper halls, and look down on ruin, ruin, ruin, all about it; the triumphal arches of Constantine, Septimius Severus, and Titus, the Roman Forum, the Palace of the Caesars, the temples of the old religion, fallen down and gone; is to see the ghost of old Rome, wicked, wonderful old city – Never in its bloodiest prime, can the sight of the gigantic Colosseum, full of lustiest life, have moved one heart as it must move all who look upon it now, a ruin.

Charles Dickens *Pictures of Italy*

●

Although there are ancient remains scattered everywhere, the great swathe of ancient Rome that now lies uncovered from the Piazza Venezia to the Colosseum can be explored in a single walk. For those who want to understand the monuments in the greatest detail, Amanda Claridge's *Rome*, in the Oxford Archaeological Guide series, is invaluable, as are the official publications of the Soprintendenza Archaeologica di Roma, which are published in several languages and are informative, beautifully illustrated and on sale at every major site and museum.

Start in the **Piazza Venezia**, a piazza dominated – many would say overwhelmed – by the unrelieved whiteness of the **Victor Emmanuel II Monument.** An equestrian statue of the king which stands at the centre was gilded at one point: the overall glare on sunny days is now almost unimaginable. This vast monument which alters the perspective of the piazza, and indeed of even the largest ancient ruins and medieval churches nearby, was inaugurated in 1911 to commemorate the dead king, Italy's first since unification. Several eminent architects and sculptors were involved in the project and perhaps this is one reason for the extraordinarily incoherent whole. Apparently randomly placed fountains, statues, steps, columns and colonnades decorate this hefty tribute to the unity of Italian nationalism. Even the names of the sculptures are weighty in a faintly old-style Eastern Bloc way: *Love for the Fatherland, Triumphal Processions of Work*. The scale is such that at its opening a dinner was held inside the bronze horse of the central statue. No ironic intention is recorded.

●

> It's a very understanding hotel. They . . . gave me the room I wanted, one with a balcony because if you have things you don't want to think about you can always look at the view and fashionably dislike the Victor Emmanuel monument though it's better than most of the crummy Roman architecture, you can see I have no taste.
>
> William Golding *The Paper Men* (1988)

●

The Tomb of the Unknown Soldier was added to the monument in 1924, when a particularly Italian feature was included in the ritual which was being performed in many other countries: here in Rome the mother of a missing soldier picked the body to be interred.

The monument as a whole has been much criticized over the decades but it does impose itself on the city in a way that ancient emperors might recognize and, in utilitarian terms, it is undeniably a landmark, visible from almost everywhere, greater even than the Colosseum, to help visitors locate themselves in a chaotic city. Today exhibitions are held inside it and, like almost every other historic monument in Rome; it has acquired its place in the artistic imagination; its dislocated and oppressive appearance offered an irresistible setting for Peter Greenaway when he was filming *The Belly of an Architect*.

●

Italians longed for Rome as Rome was. The Roman Town Council had bestowed upon them for their royal capital a paltry and spurious copy of Paris Boulevards. Nothing so pretentious, commonplace, unspiritual and dull has ever been produced as neo-regal Rome. In addition to a display of poverty of artistic ideas almost amounting to genius, the Roman municipality is, moreover, acknowledged to have set at defiance all the rules of recent sanitary science in a manner incomparably its own.

The Times (leader) 10 January 1888

●

To one side of Piazza Venezia is the sixteenth-century and seventeenth-century **Palazzo di Venezia**. Mussolini's offices were in this building and he used the open balcony to give his addresses to the crowd. Standing facing the Victor Emmanuel monument, walk up the right-hand side until you reach two flights of steps. The first – steep – one climbs to the church of **S. Maria in Aracoeli**, while the second, more gradual incline, with two statues of lions at its foot and with colossal statues of Castor and Pollux at the top, leads to the **Campidoglio**, on the site of Ancient Rome's **Capitol**. This has always been one of the most significant sites in Roman history. Here Brutus came, still with blood on his hands, to relay the news of Julius Caesar's assassination in 44 BCE, here in 1341 the poet Petrarch was crowned with laurels, here Gibbon made the decision in 1764 not to pursue his intended history of

Switzerland but to produce a history of the later Roman Empire. (Although it was subsequently shown that, accurate historian or not, the elements of inspiration as he later recorded them could never have been as he described.) And 180 years later it was here that General Mark Clark declared that Rome had been liberated from the Germans.

●

Yesterday, on June fourth, 1944, Rome fell to American and Allied troops. The first of the Axis capitals is now in our hands. One up and two to go!

It is perhaps significant that the first of these capitals to fall should have the longest history of all of them. The story of Rome goes back to the time of the foundations of our civilization. We can still see there monuments of the time when Rome and the Romans controlled the whole of the then known world. That, too, is significant, for the United Nations are determined that in the future no one city and no one race will be able to control the whole of the world.

Franklin D. Roosevelt

●

The steps climbed by Gibbon and General Clark, known as the **cordonato**, were designed by Michelangelo, as was the geometrically patterned piazza at the top. To either side are the superb **Capitoline Museums** where outstanding – and sometimes disarmingly familiar – art and sculpture are displayed in the handsome Renaissance rooms of the Palazzo Nuovo and Palazzo dei Conservatori. The statue at the centre of the piazza is one of the greatest of emperors: the philosopher Marcus Aurelius (it is a replica but the original is just inside the Palazzo Nuovo). The statue survived the destroying might of the Church where many other pagan images succumbed,

Statues of the Dioscuri, Capitoline

not because of Marcus Aurelius's considerable personal qualities (although as well as studying philosophy he was also alleged to have forced his promiscuous wife Faustina to bathe in the blood of her murdered lover) nor because of the artistic achievement of the sculptor but simply because it was mistakenly thought to be a statue of the Emperor Constantine, a Christian convert. The colossal head and other fragments of a statue that *was* of Constantine, an iconic image for Roman postcards, stand in the courtyard of the Palazzo dei Conservatori to the right. They are almost modernist in their massive and depersonalized depiction of the emperor.

The piazza is a handsome and popular space for wedding photography. Mingling with the crowds are newly sanctioned couples, often two or three of them dotted around the square outside the registry office, with attendant photographer, light-man, tripod and camera. Bare-shouldered brides with coiled hair, low bodices, wide lace skirts and slightly awkward husbands pose by statues and steps, encouraged by their photographers to hitch their dress up to show a thigh, white stocking top and garter to the camera and the milling crowds.

There are always police up here, too – invariably relaxed. One breezy evening, the small police car has four of them crammed in and is moving lightly on its springs. In the failing light a small television screen can be seen on the dashboard; the World Cup has their complete attention. On another, warmer night two policemen compete for the attentions of a third officer – a pretty blonde wearing a short skirt and the ubiquitous high heels, and with an elegant police cap perched on loose glossy hair. She is leaning back against the car, one knee raised. Even allowing for the considerable style that Romans bring to the wearing of any uniform, the footwear is a mystery. It is hard enough to walk, let alone give chase, on Rome's cobbled and potholed streets.

The free concerts in summer are one of Rome's delights. Wander up here after nine p.m. as the day finally slips away and find the Symphony Orchestra of Rome obviously enjoying themselves, performing Beethoven or Mozart or, less predictably, music from *Star Wars*, *Superman* and *Schindler's List* or, absolutely predictably, excerpts from Puccini's *Tosca* and Respighi's *The Pines of Rome*. The audience comes and goes, sitting on the steps of the museums, standing on the raised entrance to the Palazzo Senatorio at the back of the piazza, whispering, nuzzling, clapping and dozing in the warm night. Beneath the palazzo entrance, statues of the personifications of the Nile and the Tiber, bearded men of gravitas, look on, as does a statue of the goddess Roma. To the immediate left of the Palazzo a replica statue of Romulus and Remus being suckled by a scrawny wolf stands out at the top of a column and is silhouetted against the sky.

Walk a short way down this road and a marvellous view of the **Roman Forum**, the political and religious heart of ancient

Rome, unfolds. From above – and it can be seen from either side of the Palazzo Senatorio – the extraordinary if exhilarating muddle of ruins comes nearest to making sense. To the left is the Arch of **Septimius Severus**, far over to the right and covered in trees is the **Palatine Hill**.

It is possible to go into the Forum by passing down the right-hand side of the Palazzo Senatorio and taking the Via di Consolazione, which snakes right and then left down the hill; this brings you to a gate which is little used and gives instant access to the Forum over huge paving slabs of stone which the steps of history have smoothed and made lethally slippery in rain. The consolation of the street name is that offered to those enduring the traditional ancient execution of being thrown from the **Tarpeian Rock**. The drop does not look high enough to ensure that death was either certain or quick.

However, it is also possible to enter (or leave) the Forum by the well-used gate on the Via dei Fori Imperiali. To reach this, continue down the road to the left of the Palazzo Senatorio, a small cobbled street that is heavy with the smell of acanthus in May and June. To the immediate left and down some steps is the church of **S. Giuseppe dei Falegnami** and within this is the bleak and claustrophobic **Mamertine Prison** which probably dates from the fourth century BCE in construction if not in name (the Romans simply called it *carcer* – prison). Not now thought to have held St Paul after his arrest, nor indeed to have hosted his angelic visitation, many others were certainly held, shackled to the walls, in its two dark, wet rooms, one below the other, with no light or drainage, reached only by holes in their ceilings. Executions by strangulation took place in the lower cell, including that of the Gaul, Vercingetorix. Other condemned prisoners were taken from here to be thrown off the Tarpeian Rock. Probably the prison was at rather than below ground level at the time when it was constructed.

It is a shame that in their haste to see this grisly relic so many people pass by the church itself; its name means St Joseph of the Carpenters and, for a small church, it has a surprisingly fine carved wooden ceiling, wooden nativity scene and a small chapel which once served the carpenters' guild.

The small street comes out behind the Victor Emmanuel II Monument and immediately across the road here are various imperial markets. Far and away the best of these are **Trajan's Markets**, visible from the road to the left and substantially more intact than other ruins here. These are not in fact a single construction but two storeys of small shops and storage rooms that are quite recognizable to anyone who has shopped in a modern shopping centre.

Trajan's Column can be seen further to the left, back towards Piazza Venezia. The column was the first official archaeological site in Rome. It commemorates the CE second-century Emperor Trajan and where the statue of St Peter standing on the top now claims the city for Christianity, one of Trajan himself in full military dress once looked out over Rome at the height of its imperial power. Like most surviving monuments, the column was pressed into subsequent service, in this case as a bell tower to the now demolished S. Nicola de Columna. Its helical frieze is a bit of a mystery; it portrays the emperor's military campaigns in extraordinary detail, so much so that it has been a major source of information for military historians. Nevertheless, it cannot be seen clearly in situ; for that it is necessary either to travel out to EUR and the Museum of Roman Civilization or to London where copies – of some of it, at least – are displayed unrolled.

From this point the Colosseum is unmistakable. Walk towards it and on the right-hand side of Via dei Fori Imperiali is the main entrance to the Forum.

The remnants of buildings central to the stories of ancient Roman history and culture have been excavated, buildings known to perhaps a hundred subsequent generations from Latin literature and history: the Temple of the Divine Julius where Julius Caesar was cremated after his assassination, the House of the Vestal Virgins, the Curia, official seat of the Senate, the Rostra from which Roman politicians addressed the people. These are not necessarily buildings which existed contemporaneously but, rather, are the product of centuries of political and mercantile life; yet excavation has to a degree rendered them all apparently of an age.

Trajan's Column

For perjurers try the Comitium. Liars and braggarts hang round the Shrine of Cloacina; rich, married ne'er-do-wells by the Basilica. Packs of prostitutes there too – but rather clapped-out ones. In the Fish Market members of dining clubs. In the Lower Forum respectable well-to-do citizens out for a stroll; in the Middle Forum, flashier types, along the canal. By the Lacus Curtius you'll find bold fellows with a tongue in their head and a bad intent in their mind – great slanderers of others and very vulnerable to it themselves. By the old shops, the money-lenders, they'll make or take a loan. Behind the Temple of Castor, there are men to whom you wouldn't entrust yourself. In the Vicus Tuscus are men who sell themselves.

Plautus Curculio

There are three kinds of sightseer in the Roman Forum. Groups with tour leaders cluster in what little shade there is, more or less alert to the information and anecdotes being relayed in French, German, Japanese, English or Italian. The serious seekers after knowledge quarter the ruins, archaeological guide in hand, their eyes on floor plans and sketched reconstructions, identifying each relic from the *tabularium* to the House of the Vestals, the *cloaca maxima* to the *rostra*; they are perhaps the modern-day counterpart to earlier travellers who clambered rapturously over the then even less comprehensible ruins, clutching their Cicero or Tacitus.

Roman refreshment

A third group are more like the nineteenth-century romantics in their approach, wandering haphazardly around broken columns, worn paving slabs and sturdy carved arches, resting under oleanders, simply absorbing the weight of history and reflecting happily on the transitory nature of all things.

Both the Forum and the Colosseum had a slightly sinister reputation in the past. Excavation was held to stir up all manner of illness and Rome itself was associated with moral contagion. Poor Daisy Miller, eponymous heroine of Henry James's book, has a rendezvous with an Italian admirer in the Colosseum by night and catches the illness that kills her.

Even now, the ruins are not devoid of potent associations. When Benjamin Netanyahu came to Rome as Prime Minister of Israel he asked to be allowed to enter the site during hours when it was closed expressly for the purpose of walking under the **Arch of Titus** on which the destruction of the Temple in Jerusalem and the sacking of its treasures are depicted. Equally, it is widely believed, although disputed by many scholars, that Christians being thrown to the lions was a major spectacle in the Colosseum and a large cross still marks the site of these supposed early martyrdoms.

●

She stood up and leaned against the parapet, filling her troubled eyes with the tranquillizing magic of the hour. But instead of tranquillizing her the sight seemed to increase her exasperation. Her gaze turned to the Colosseum. Already its golden flank was drowned in purple shadow, and above it the sky curved crystal clear, without light or colour. It was the moment when afternoon and evening hang balanced in mid-heaven.

Mrs Slade turned back and laid her hand on her friend's arm. The gesture was so abrupt that Mrs Ansley looked up, startled.

'The sun's set. You're not afraid, my dear?'
'Afraid—?'
'Of Roman fever or pneumonia—?'

Edith Wharton Roman Fever

•

The Forum is best visited out of high season. Not only is it less crowded – in June and July it may be as teeming as it was two thousand years earlier – but the lack of shade can make the crossing of its paving stones and fractured marble an experience where heat and the complexity of the endless vista of ruins combine to make a dizzying whole.

Whatever time or season it is, the mood is calmer and the temperature cooler on the **Palatine**. The path through the Forum turns sharp right to pass in front of the unmistakable landmark of the Arch of Titus and right again, above and alongside the ruined **House of the Vestals**, to a tiny ticket office. While entry to the Forum is free, now an inalienable right of heritage, there is a charge for entry to the Palatine, the hill of the emperors and the aristocracy. Only a fraction of the numbers who clamber around the Forum persevere up to the Palatine, yet they all seem to get to the tiny ticket office at once. This is a new system, replacing the simple old turnstile with a new bottleneck. On a busy day in June, the height of the season, the temperature is rising fast and there is no shade for the queue outside. Only one man on duty, a perplexing list of ticket combinations which raise questions from one or two purchasers – and no change. A fact not relayed to those at the back, queuing, as it were, in vain, notes in hot hands.

Still, the Palatine is worth seeing at any cost. Or not so much worth seeing as worth being on. It is a green and peaceful hill, where the quiet ruins are surrounded by gardens. In fact, the more formal areas of beautifully laid out upper terraces

Ruins of the Palatine

above the current entrance are the Renaissance gardens of the Farnese family. A cool and evocative nymphaeum survives with its damp green walls and statues and so does a lush grotto where water trickles down a deep cleft of rock, thick with accretions of moss and fern, and patters into a clear pool below.

Excavations have shown that the Palatine was one of the first areas to be colonized in Rome, in around the eighth and ninth century BCE, and it is the traditional site of the birthplace of Romulus and Remus. Up here one can understand why it became the location of choice for the houses of the imperial family and the patricians. We even get the word 'palace' from the name of this hill, with its uninterrupted views of the city and of the daily traffic between the leisurely life of the heights and the business of the Forum below for those who once lived here. The topography of the hill that we see today – actually best viewed driving or walking along the far side of the **Circus Maximus**, where it looms implacably over the old stadium **(Walk 6)** – is largely man-made. What survives are the massive foundations and buttressing that allowed the emperors to expand their palace complexes. Although there are traces of structures of every age up here, including sunken gardens, racetracks, temples, baths, cemeteries, and even Iron Age huts, the most substantial ruins are those of the palace of the much-feared Emperor Domitian. His paranoia and cruelty shaped his reign; he was said (by his not-unpartisan biographers) to spend hours stabbing flies with a pen while his secret agents, more lethally, prowled the streets stabbing passers-by with venom-tipped needles. All this came to a bloody end in CE 96 when Domitian was himself stabbed to death in his own bedroom, by members of his own inner circle, within this palace. A palace that had itself become as notorious and feared as its emperor.

He prepared a room that was pitch black on every side, ceiling, walls and floor, and had made ready bare couches of the same colour resting on the uncovered floor; then he invited his guests in without their attendants. And first he set beside each of them a slab shaped like a gravestone, bearing the guest's name and also a small lamp such as hanging in tombs.

Cassius Dio *Roman History* VIII, bk 67

Archaeological analysis has revealed that the palace did indeed have forbidding proportions, a nexus of rooms as high as they were wide. On late-summer evenings sudden storms blow in across the city and black clouds roll towards the Palatine, spitting heavy drops of rain. On such days **Domitian's Palace**, whose three-feet-thick walls have survived time, is one of the few places to offer shelter.

Also up here the so-called **House of Livia** has fine examples of CE first-century wall paintings and the cryptoporticus – a subterranean passage that connected different parts of the Palatine complex with each other – runs along the south-west corner. The roof is now partly open above, providing a view of the long cool corridor, but visitors can usually, although not always, gain entry to walk along inside it.

●

We climbed the magnificent Palatine hill, where the magnificent Palace of the emperors stood. Since it has suffered many changes, we must believe that the ruins we now see date from the time of Domitian . . . we walked to where the house of Cicero was and I was seized with enthusiasm. I began to speak Latin.

Boswell on the Grand Tour:
Italy, Corsica, France 1765–1766

●

Walk back down the Palatine and across the Forum to the gate on the Via dei Fori Imperiali and turn right. There, spread across the road, like an impassable wall, is the **Colosseum**. In Rome the approach to a major tourist attraction is marked by a proliferation of stalls selling reproductions of great artworks of the classical world. Plastic or resin, pagan or Christian, Roman or Greek: these are the places, second only to the Vatican, for the lover of kitsch. The synaptic spark between the finger of God and Man on the Sistine Chapel ceiling is reproduced on aprons, mugs, postcards and T-shirts. So are the colours of the Roma and Lazio football teams. Here are snowstorm globes of St Peter's, a snowstorm Augustus holding up his hand in the style of Canute, snowstorm Trajan's Columns, snowstorm Colosseums and, indeed, snowstorm Parthenons. The Parthenon is selling well. Someone with a heavy hand for computer graphics has produced the somehow disturbing image of a Colosseum filled to the brim with spaghetti pomodoro. The pasta looks like entrails.

There are vans selling iced water, ice creams and pistachios, and a coconut seller, his slabs of fresh-broken coconut kept cool in flowing water. There are gypsy women in cheerful flowered fabrics and with wary, resigned faces, begging with their babies, hawkers waiting for strolling payers to buy sunglasses or hand-held fans. Market forces operate like magic here; the speed with which the wares are switched to umbrellas and plastic hoods if a shower appears on the horizon is admirable.

○

Cars and spluttering vespas circled the Colosseum as I attempted to cross the street into the shadowy old building, more a city than a building, more a tall ship than a city, a ship leaning into the watery moon and the racing ermine clouds and with most of the sailors down below in the hold.

Edmund White *The Farewell Symphony* (1997)

○

On a wall to the right of the Via dei Fori Imperiali, in front of the Colosseum, are four metal **maps of the Roman Empire** from its beginnings until its second-century prime. They are informative and impressive and are a reminder that the Roman Empire cannot be reduced merely to picturesque ruins.

Long before you reach the Colosseum the gladiators start to appear. Or are they legionaries? (In the public perception nothing distinguishes the two.) Worked-out bronzed bodies, gilt breastplates and shin-guards, thonged sandals and polyester red skirts shining in the sun. They clunk about in

'Gladiators', Colosseum

twos and threes; the city authorities have begun to control their enterprise and have prohibited plastic armour in favour of something closer to the real thing. Whatever that might be. While one in sunglasses snatches a furtive cigarette on a bench, two others bear down on a group of German schoolchildren. Prices have been fixed too; there is a limit now on how much they can charge for adorning a tourist photograph. Occasionally there's a spat about a pitch; pushing and shoving, more a harmless if noisy clash of cymbals or a lumbering collision of mating tortoises than the actions of Russell Crowe at his most introspectively muscular.

Out-of-work actors, out-of-jail crooks. Not a lot different from the old days.

If the Colosseum is the iconic building of Rome then the all-purpose Ancient Roman fighting man is the iconic figure. They are spreading. Now there are gladiators sparring and posing around the early-twentieth-century Victor Emmanuel II Monument and the baroque Spanish Steps. It is not just a matter of a tourist rip-off either, but of national identity: helmeted gladiators are a popular choice for tattoos and a gladiator school down the Appian Way is teaching the old skills to Roman plasterers and computer programmers and is staging fight reconstructions. The real ancient gladiator barracks and training school, the **Ludus Magnus**, has been excavated just a short distance south of the Colosseum itself. It is on the junction of Via di Labicana and Via di S. Giovanni Laterano, several feet below today's city level.

The queue for the Colosseum is long, only here, unlike the equally daunting lines at the Vatican, the queuing is done in the shade of the arcades. The word for 'arch' in Latin is *fornix* and the prevalence of prostitutes in ancient Rome, hanging around under the arenas' arches waiting for post-games trade, gave us the word 'fornication'. None of that here now, though other traditional sites – the Baths of Caracalla, the Appian Way – still see an old trade.

The interior of the Colosseum *is* impressive: the tiers are dizzyingly high, the mechanics of the whole slick operation – the hydraulics, the animal pens, the lifts – are now exposed, but as a feat of engineering rather than the logistics of drama, courage and blood. And at the highest level swallows still dip and soar over the arena. For the only passingly curious, much of the interior can be spied through the arches and it is the building seen from the outside in the context of the city that is really unforgettable. Queuing is not mandatory.

Beside the Colosseum is the third of the three surviving triumphal arches of Rome, arches built to celebrate the glory of an emperor or of a general returning from a successful and profitable war. This one is the **Arch of Constantine**. The other two are those of Septimius Severus and of Titus, both of which are in the Forum.

It *is* worth queuing for entrance to the **Domus Aurea**, Nero's Golden House, deep in the hill opposite. Cross the road beyond the Colosseum and climb to the small park above the pavement. This is the **Colle Oppio**. On its road side it is a pretty park of flower beds, paths and the occasional statue. To the rear it is a slightly less relaxed place to linger, although this is mostly because down-and-outs and the homeless have taken up semi-residence on its benches.

Various ancient buildings, including the infamous Golden House, once a vast complex of

Nero's Golden House

rooms and magnificent gardens, lie under this park. The **Domus Aurea** is to the left-hand side as you face the park. When the flamboyantly capricious Nero was toppled and forced to kill himself, the Flavian emperors who eventually succeeded him built a great circular amphitheatre on the site of his property, obliterating his ornamental lake, to make a flamboyant point of returning it to the people. Ironically, the amphitheatre acquired the name 'Colosseum', not because of its own size but because of the colossal gold statue of Nero himself, naked, which had once stood in that position but which was now given a new head and a new identity as the Sun God (the first of several identities: it subsequently became Hercules, and then the Sun God again, before disappearing from the record).

Quandiu stat Colisaeus, stat et Roma; quando cadet Colisaeus, cadet et Roma. Quando cadet Roma, cadet et mundus.

As long as the Colossus stands, Rome stands; when the Colossus falls, Rome will fall. When Rome falls, the world will fall.

Venerable Bede, eighth century CE

Meanwhile one storey of a wing of Nero's palace had survived, forgotten for one and a half millennia, under the foundations of the later **Baths of Trajan**. Even Nero's ghost had not returned here but chose instead to haunt the Piazza del Popolo. From the late sixteenth century, as the superstructure collapsed in places, areas within the Domus started to be discovered by travellers; indeed, the impression made on them by the wall decorations inside meant that their style, copied by passing artists, became the fashion of the age in the grand houses of Europe. Irrigation of the park subsequently damaged much of the decoration and these early copies are one of the principal sources of information. The wing was excavated properly from the nineteenth century onward but was only opened, in part, to the public in the last couple of years.

Buying an entrance ticket seems slightly complicated but is designed to limit the numbers entering at one time. After a visit to the box office you are given a time to return, usually half an hour or so later. Turning left outside the entrance walk along the path between rose beds and in two minutes you will come to one of Rome's traditional old coffee stalls, a dark green polygonal wooden kiosk set under the trees where a very old lady in a chintz overall serves espresso plus cold drinks, bars of chocolate and little pastries. Mothers and babies, a park keeper and his girlfriend, an old man and his dog all sit at metal tables scattered around. It is a very gentle, very Roman scene; a perfect place to wait before a visit to Nero.

A visit to the Domus Aurea must always be guided. There is no wandering off to muse alone in these dark passages and vaults. The degree of information that you receive is up to you – there are different options – but even the short guided tour is quite educational. Talking in English as well as Italian, the guide knows her stuff and without her it would be easy to miss some of the highlights of this strange ruin. There are 150 rooms known here, of which only a fraction allow public access. For much of the walk it is like passing through a series of prehistoric caves in the constant coolness – take a jumper, even at the height of summer – with the rough floor and rubble-blocked side passages; but occasionally the hand of (bad) man is clearly visible and surprisingly poignant. The decorated floors, the artificial stalactites in the grotto, the delicate wall paintings of mythical scenes of war and reconciliation, of fruit and birds, of sea scenes with dolphins and marine life, and *trompe l'œil* effects of marbles and draperies, are reminders that this whole complex was once rich in precious materials, especially coloured marbles and gilding. That a real person lived here. It was once, above all, with its great windows and open colonnades, a place of light and playing water.

●

Parts of the house were overlaid with gold and studded with precious stones and mother-of-pearl. All the dining rooms had ceilings of fretted ivory, the panels of which could slide back and let a rain of flowers, or of perfume from hidden sprinklers, shower upon his guests. The main dining room was circular and its roof revolved, day and night, in time with the sky.

Suetonius *The Twelve Caesars*:
Nero (second century CE)

When you leave the Domus, come out of the park towards the Colosseum. Walk back along the climbing upper path and turn right up the side of the park along a little road called Via Terme di Tito. There are – inevitably – many restaurants in the area around the Colosseum. Many, though not all, combine high prices and indifferent service. The restaurant by the Metro station is particularly to be avoided. But up the Via Terme di Tito there is one real delight: *Osteria da Nerone*. Ignoring all the tourist frenzy, the squabbling accordionists and the hungry but uncertain passers-by, this is simply a friendly restaurant serving proper Roman food with charm and a slightly old-fashioned air. Sit under the plane trees at a table on the pavement and face the challenge of a plate filled from *Osteria da Nerone*'s superb self-service hot-and-cold table. The chef – and his elderly mother – are inclined to hover, giving a running commentary on your choices and suggesting their favourite dishes, and outside another son of the family is as smiling and patient as if he were presiding over an osteria in a sleepy provincial town.

Beyond *Osteria da Nerone*, tour buses disgorge the hot and confused of many nations; at the bottom of the road it is back to the smirking tough-guy gladiators or to the **Colosseo** Metro station and another descent into the dark.

●

Good, now I can at last begin to live like a human being!

Nero, on taking possession of the *Domus Aurea*.
Quoted by Suetonius in *The Twelve Caesars: Nero*

●

WALK 5

The Via Nomentana

- Porta Pia
- Churches of S. Agnese Fuori Le Mura and S. Constanza
- Catacombs of S. Agnese and Priscilla
- Villa Torlonia
- Casina della Civette
- Peroni Brewery and Museum of Contemporary Art
- Quartier Dora
- Via Salaria
- Villa Ada
- Forte Antenne
- Ponte Nomentana
- Monte Sacro

The Via Nomentana is a long, wide and busy avenue leading north-east out of the city through moderately prosperous suburbs. The big houses, apartment buildings and embassies to each side are, in the main, of nineteenth- and twentieth-century origin. These are solid, well-established households, organizational headquarters and embassies set in large, well-kept gardens. But Via Nomentana is a far, far older road than it appears. It was one of the principal Ancient Roman highways, and exploration here reveals some venerable gems, dignified and beautiful in their simplicity, as well as one or two more recent spectacular bursts of eccentricity which prove that Rome need not always be a place of exemplary aestheticism. But Via Nomentana and the area between it and **Via Salaria**, an equally venerable highway, also possess fine public parks, many with summer festivals and exhibitions.

Porta Pia

This is an exploration that can be undertaken by car or on foot. If you have a car it is worth driving out through the city gate of the **Porta Pia** where the entry of Garibaldi and his troops on 7 September 1870 made Rome part of a united Italy. The gate itself was designed by Michelangelo and was his last work, completed in 1561. Again, with a car it is possible to

Ponte Nomentana

S. *Agnese Fuori Le Mura*

follow Via Nomentana all the way out to the **Ponte Nomentana** which crosses a tributary of the Tiber at **Monte Sacro**. It is still a picture-book medieval bridge, and was much favoured by the Grand Tourists as a subject of sketches or the background to portraits.

But plenty can be seen simply on foot. To walk, start at the church of **S. Agnese Fuori Le Mura** (St Agnes outside the Walls) at Via Nomentana 349. Either take the Metro to the Bologna station and walk west or take the tram/bus from Termini and ask to be told where to get off for the church.

Pass through the gateway and you travel back 1,300 years, entering a peaceful enclave of early Christian buildings. **The Church and Catacombs of S. Agnese Fuori Le Mura**, the **Mausoleum of Constantia** and the ruins of a huge basilica stand among gardens, gravel walks and shrines. It has a very special, peaceful atmosphere. On 21 April, the feast day of Saint Agnes, lambs are brought to be blessed in this church before being handed over to the care of the nuns of **S. Cecilia in Trastevere (Walk 8)** where they will stay until they are ceremonially shorn and their fleece made into a *pallium*, the white cloak given by the Pope to new archbishops. Reservations can be made to take part in this ancient service.

The interior of the lovely church is reached down a broad flight of shallow steps. Originally the seventh-century building was built into the subterranean cemetery and to either side of the steps ancient fragments and funerary inscriptions, many quite beautiful, several still clearly legible, have been retrieved and mounted on the walls. Inside, the church has, unusually, a woman's gallery above the nave. It also has a very fine mosaic in the apse in which the thirteen-year-old Saint Agnes's extended and gruesome torture and martyrdom (allegedly in the **Stadium of Domitian**, the present site of **S. Agnese in Agone**) is reduced to the depiction of some small flames and a sword. In the mosaic she rises resplendent, dressed and bejewelled as a Byzantine empress. Her body lies beneath the altar of the church and can be seen in its coffin by taking the door to the right as you face the altar.

•

> Golden painting comes out of the enamels and daylight both embraces and is confined. Dawn might think of plunging out of snow-white springs into the clouds, watering the fields with her dews: here is such a light as even the rainbow will produce between the stars or the purple peacock bright with colour. God who might bring an end to night or light has banished chaos from here out of the tomb of the martyrs.

> Dedication to the seventh-century Honorious I
> in the apse of S Agnese Fuori

•

Also under the church are seven kilometres of catacombs on many levels. A small proportion of these are open to the public. Unlike in the better-known catacombs on the Appian Way **(Walk 10)**, individual visitors may find themselves alone in these cool dim tunnels with only an enthusiastic young guide, who turns right and left without hesitation, spinning out the light of her torch, revealing row after row of the niches known as *loculi* where the dead were interred. These catacombs were not, as some believe, a place where Christians held secret services. There is an inscription here, some small bones there and an oil-lamp holder and a smoky smudge on the stone beside many burials, while galleries and arches lead away into an unknown and labyrinthine darkness. No beautiful frescoes adorn these catacombs: these are the simple graves of ordinary people in their thousands, but in some ways they are more touching because of it. Whole sections are of tiny *loculi* that once held, and sometimes still do, the remains of children, a reminder of the rate of child mortality in ancient and medieval cities. Others have rough drawings indicating the profession of the deceased: a fat *prosciutto*, no different to those hams hanging in the shops and markets of Rome today, indicates a butcher, a man posing with a shovel was himself a gravedigger. Rudimentary etched drawings of doves and fish and saints speak of a religion still in its infancy.

Back in the sun and across a flower-filled courtyard there is a small rock grotto with a plaster saint and row upon row of votive objects, mostly hearts hung on ribbons, some with silver still bright and hopeful, others tarnished with time. There are photographs, painfully often of children, prayers, intercessions and notes of thanks. A young woman sits on a bench facing the Virgin, her head bowed, waiting.

Mausoleum of Constantia

To the left, down a short avenue, is the tomb of Constantia, the daughter of the Roman Emperor Constantine. Her resting place, built in about CE 351, is a circular mausoleum of graceful beauty, now one of Rome's most appealing churches (dedicated, strangely, and presumably in error, to a nun, S. Costanza). Natural light is filtered through the fretwork of twelve windows high in a central dome, and a circular colonnade is supported by twelve slender granite columns. The uncluttered internal space is cool and calm. It is a thousand years from the busy elaboration of Rome's ubiquitous baroque. There is an appealing contrast between the simple curves of the building and the rich and delicate fourth-century mosaics in gold and jewel-like colours that cover the lower ceiling. Some of these are geometric patterns, some are fantasies: gardens with peacocks, songbirds, grapes, pomegranates and flowers, flasks and musical instruments. Others are rural scenes of winemaking (they are decidedly pagan, not Christian, images) and at their centre is a picture of Constantia and her first husband Annibaliano. Constantia's splendid red sarcophagus is a replica; the original is in the Vatican museums.

●

I went yesterday to the little church on the Via Nomentana. The Milizia – hand-picked boys, all very handsome in black, lined the entrance and when the bridal couple left the church they walked under their daggers, the only weapons they carry, and made an arch . . . The President of the Senate and everyone in Black Shirts and their decorations. The bride arrived alone in the car with the Duce.

Julia Brambilla, *Rome in the 1930s*:
Jottings from Julia's Journal (1965)

●

Turning right out of the main gate, cross the road and go back in the direction of central Rome. After ten minutes' walk the gates of **Villa Torlonia** appear at Via Nomentana 70. Villa Torlonia is still undergoing restoration but its park is open to the public and its extraordinary follies and decoration are scattered all over its grounds. Giovanni

Torlonia (1755–1829) was the founder of a banking dynasty and his aim in building his villa was to equal or exceed the grand houses of the aristocracy. He hired the architect Valadier to design it and work continued under subsequent members of the family for eighty years. Torlonia and his if anything more eccentric heir added numerous architectural features within his estate, including obelisks, a castle, a temple, a Moorish villa, an amphitheatre, a lake, ruins and a cave. All are now in some degree of dilapidation but rescue work has begun to retrieve this unique collection of buildings. As with so many buildings along the Via Nomentana, the site chosen was, unknown to the builders, on top of an extensive range of catacombs, in this case Jewish ones. These were only discovered in the twentieth century, when the richness of their Hebraic motifs and decoration was exposed. The catacombs are not yet open to the public.

During the war Mussolini rented the villa from an obliging Torlonia for a token one lira a year and used a portion of the catacombs as an air-raid shelter. After the war Allied military occupation of the whole complex accelerated a process of decay, but it has recently been decided that the neoclassical villa will, appropriately, become a museum of the Holocaust in Italy.

However, pending the reopening of the Villa itself the main reason to come to Villa Torlonia is to visit one of the more bizarre manifestations of Torlonia taste. The newly restored **Casina delle Civette (Owl Pavilion)** was built by Giovanni's strange nephew, Prince Giovanni Torlonia. It is famed for reflecting the prince's alleged love of the occult but the carved stone snails, the snakes and the flight of little bats across the prince's bedroom ceiling increase an effect of whimsy rather than create a sinister atmosphere. For the Casina is beyond architectural classification. 'Eclectic' does not begin to cover it. It is somewhere between a Swiss chalet, a small Bavarian castle

Casina della Civette, Villa Torlonia

and the sort of house made of sweets, potentially inhabited by a dubious old woman, that wandering children might be well advised to stay away from. It has turrets, shiny green majolica roof tiles, wooden balconies, mosaic pavements, fluted stone columns and Dutch gables. Begun in 1840 as a rustic Alpine hut, expanded as a medieval house in 1908, used as a principal dwelling by the prince and later occupied by the Anglo-American Command from 1944–7, it was derelict when rescued by the state in 1978.

Today the restored – and unique – art-nouveau interior has an odd charm. Wood and glass have been worked by master craftsmen of the period; greys, greens, pinks and purples predominate. Stairs are lit by overhead windows that have a design of bluebirds, a tiny circular panelled room has both its cupola ceiling and a wooden settle embellished with Torlonia's favourite snail motif, stained-glass roses climb up French windows and are mirrored by the real ones growing over the portico; tendrils of vines and flights of butterflies and owls fill the panes. Small exhibitions of modern art are held here, and there is a museum of stained glass with examples, drawings and explanations of techniques, as well as a small, well-arranged architectural library.

The staff at Roman museums and tourist sights almost invariably fall into one of two groups: the wearily indifferent and the chattering enthusiastic. The Casina's band of rather elegantly dressed late-middle-aged female custodians form another category. They are more like new acquaintances, gently tapping you on the arm to suggest that you go this way or that, examine this detail, see this window in just this light, come into this room, turn round to capture an unexpected view. Impossible not to believe that they are volunteers: 'Friends of the Owl Pavilion' or some such. Concerts are held here in summer: they too are eclectic, covering everything from the songs of Lennon and McCartney to Jerome Kern, Beethoven symphonies to Schubert's string quartets and selections from Verdi's *La Traviata*.

From Villa Torlonia turn left. There is yet more to explore in the world of nineteenth- and early twentieth-century architectural innovation. Continue up Via Nomentana as far as the busy crossroads with Viale Regina Margherita. Continue over this and the second turning to the right is Via Reggio Emilia, where the art deco **Peroni Brewery** has been turned into the **Museum of Contemporary Art of Rome**, with the acronym **MACRO**. It is just that too far away from the city centre to attract the attendance it deserves, although an annexe in the old abattoir in Trastevere (**Walk 8**) at Piazza Orazio Giustiniani 4 is also worth seeing – and easier to get to.

Typical Roman street sign

Turn back (facing away from central Rome) to the Nomentana/Regina Margherita crossroads and then turn left. Either walk or take almost any bus or tram two stops to Piazza Buenos Aires, north-west of Via Nomentana, and then go along the little Via Anaro at the south-eastern side of the piazza and walk on to Piazza Mincio. This is a small area officially called the **Quartier Dora** but more often known as **Coppedé**, after an architect who was ground-breaking not so much in his rejection as in his all-encompassing inclusion of existing architectural conventions. Coppedé developed these streets in the 1920s and they still have a period feel even as modern life hurries on within them. In style they have echoes of Casina della Civette, both in their rapturous embrace of decoration and in a certain lack of grace: medieval-style towers rise from rugged rustic lower courses, triumphal arches have accretions of grotesque heads, hefty porches are lined with gold and blue cloisonné, while mythical creatures and foliage, Assyrian and Babylonian and Egyptian motifs,

Art Noveau excesses at Coppedé at Piazza Mincio

encrust every building, particularly around the Piazza Mincio with its charming but decidedly kitsch fountain of frogs. Here too are a cluster of three houses known as the Fairy Villas. (Further work by Coppedé may be seen in the Via Veneto. The **Palazzo Coppedé** at Via Veneto 7 was designed in 1927, the year of Coppedé's death, with his signature eccentricities, in this case a monkey and a particularly discomfiting Medusa over the main entrance.)

From Piazza Pincio take Via Rubicon which comes swiftly out into **Via Salaria**, another of Rome's ancient highways. Via Salaria gets its name from the crucial trade in salt. Bear right along Via Salaria, passing Rome's largest park, **Villa Ada**, on the left. The park, 450 acres of trees and gentle landscaping, offers numerous diversions, from canoeing to free gym classes around the lake, to bike or pony hire and jogging tracks, although most visitors simply wander, read, embrace or sleep. Villa Ada hosts hugely popular music festivals each year, with artists and bands from all over the world, under the banner *Roma Incontra il Mondo* (Rome meets the world). Tickets are around eight euros. For the energetic the **Forte Antenne**, at the northern tip of the park, is a nineteenth-century defensive fort, built to protect the newly united Italy but constructed on an ancient site – this mound overlooking the Tiber has always been strategically important. Today it is a rather dark and Gothic ruin, covered with vegetation and surrounded by pine woods.

Drinking fountain

However, the most famous reason to come here is found where the eastern side of the park abuts Via Salaria. At Via Salaria 430 are the **Catacombs of Priscilla**, arguably Rome's finest catacombs, not least because of their size and their outstanding frescoes. Here it is not cheerful postgraduates who escort visitors through the dark galleries but equally knowledgeable and, in their quiet way, equally enthusiastic English-speaking nuns. The interments here were also of rather grander clientele than those under S. Agnese and include several early popes. Over 40,000 *loculi*, some still sealed with their original marble slabs, contain the remains of Christians from the second century. The frescoes tell Biblical stories and include a representation of the Virgin Mary, dating from the third century, which may be the oldest known image of her (if it *is* her, and not ecclesiastical wishful thinking as some scholars believe). However fine they may be, it is not ultimately the frescoes that linger in the memory but the simple inscriptions, which have the capacity to make nearly two-thousand-year-old emotions seem immediate. A shoe-maker has written *dulce* (gentle), on the grave of his eight-year-old daughter Dora and the 'L' is formed in the shape of a little boot.

A gaunt Franciscan friar, with a wild bright eye, was our only guide, down into this profound and dreadful place. The narrow ways and openings hither and thither, coupled with the dead and heavy air, soon blotted out, in all of us, any recollection of the track by which we had come: and I could not help thinking 'Good Heaven, if, in a sudden fit of madness, he should dash the torches out, or if he should be seized with a fit, what would become of us!' On we wandered, among martyrs' graves: passing great subterranean vaulted roads, diverging in all directions, and choked up with heaps of stones.

Charles Dickens *Pictures of Italy*

Coming out of the Catacombs, turn right and take the bus back to the centre of Rome. To the left the ancient Via Salaria continues on across the Tiber.

WALK 6

The Aventine and Testaccio

- Theatre of Marcellus
- S. Nicola in Carcere
- Church and Oratory of S. Giovanni Decollato
- Piazza Bocca della Verità
- Republican temples
- S. Maria in Cosmedin
- Circus Maximus
- The Rose Garden of Rome
- Parco Savello
- S. Sabina
- Piazza dei Cavalieri di Malta
- Covered markets
- The Pyramid of Cestius
- The Protestant Cemetery
- The British Military Cemetery
- Monte Testaccio

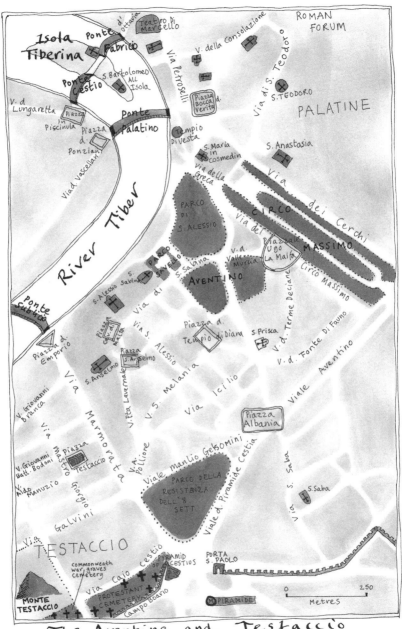

The Aventine and Testaccio

The Aventine Hill is reached on foot within ten minutes of central Rome, yet, like so many of the city hills, it has a very different atmosphere from the *centro storico*. It is a quiet, largely residential area of cool, tree-lined streets and small parks with very few restaurants and cafés. It has some of Rome's most dignified and lovely early churches and an extraordinary square designed by Piranesi.

On the far side of the hill the leafy streets descend to Testaccio, an area just outside the ancient city wall and a complete contrast to the leafy gentility of the Aventine. Testaccio has some Fascist architecture, which includes the main-line station, an ancient man-made hill, a pyramid, a large covered food market, an abandoned slaughterhouse, metal workshops, artists' and craft studios and clubs and bars which pulse distantly until the early hours. It is old in history, young in spirit, and still dominated by Romans rather than tourists, particularly those locals who are in pursuit of good food.

The Aventine Hill

The walk starts at the southern end of the **Teatro di Marcello** where, proceeding south down the main road, the Via Petroselli, there are **Fascist-era buildings** to either side. On the Tiber side of the Via del Teatro di Marcello, the little church of **S. Nicola in Carcere** on the corner of the main road and Via del Foro Olitorio (the Vegetable Market) stands on the site of three pagan temples. Beyond it, clinging on to an uncompromising run of 1930s administration blocks, is a single surviving medieval house: **Casa Crescenzia**, dating from the very early twelfth century. Across the road are ongoing excavations of further temples. A little beyond these, turn left up the Via della Misericordia to find one of Rome's secret beauties among its churches: the **Church and Oratory of S. Giovanni Decollato** (St John the Beheaded).

S. Giovanni remains a secret because it is still home to a community of nuns and is rarely open; indeed, its exterior is so implacable that it is hard to believe that its doors have not shut for ever. Yet for those fortunate few who arrive in Rome in late June, they *do* open to reveal the sixteenth-century world within. They do so for elaborate and solemn candlelit services on the saint's feast day (24 June) and for a day or so during that week when volunteers provide an excellent amount of information and cheery nuns bustle about proudly.

●

I heard of this on the Friday evening, and saw the bills up at the churches, calling on the people to pray for the criminal's soul. So, I determined to go, and see him executed. The beheading was appointed for fourteen and a-half o'clock, Roman time: or a quarter before nine in the forenoon. I had two friends with me; and as we did not know but that the crowd might be very great, we were on the spot by half-past seven. The place of execution was near the church of San Giovanni Decollato (a doubtful compliment to Saint

John the Baptist) in one of the impassable back streets without any footway, of which a great part of Rome is composed – a street of rotten houses, which do not seem to belong to anybody, and do not seem to have ever been inhabited, and certainly were never built on any plan, or for any particular purpose, and have no window-sashes, and are a little like deserted breweries, and might be warehouses but for having nothing in them.

Charles Dickens *Pictures of Italy*

●

It is an extraordinary place. The Confraternity of S. Giovanni Decollato was dedicated to the solace of condemned prisoners. The black-cowled brothers visited them in their last hours, accompanied them to the scaffold, and saw to the burial of their bodies, often within the church. The interment pits, their lids decorated with an incised tumble of skulls, bones and worms, and still with inset lever holes, lie along the peaceful cloister. Six pits for men, one for women. Several of the executed were heretics condemned by the Papal Inquisition. The cloister contains an ancient well and a pretty little garden, obviously loved. Splashes of red geranium, hydrangeas in pots and purple hollyhocks are scattered between small olive, bay and lemon trees and brick paths. There are butterflies and, somewhere unseen, doves. There are also some beautiful decorated memorials from the early sixteenth century, which are not only fine examples of the funerary art of the period, complete with small demons and skulls, but which also provide an attractive illustration of the costume of upper-class Romans of the time.

Inside, the church smells more sinister but it is only the mould and staleness of shut-up churches everywhere. The oratory is particularly fine with mannerist frescoes, again from the early sixteenth century and mostly the work of Florentine painters.

Today the order still works with prisoners, supporting their families, attempting to improve their conditions. The nuns, in modern blue habits, are social workers. They pile out of their mini-van outside, smile and say good morning as they pass under the numerous representations of decapitated heads. Repeated everywhere in paintings and carvings, over doorways, adorning the confessional, under windows, the decoration is the stuff of early horror films.

Turn right out of the church and down this short road to come into the **Piazza Bocca della Verità**. The area between the piazza and the river was once a centre of trade, with an important harbour and cattle market, but lost its sense of character and cohesion when it was cleared of many of its older buildings in the Fascist era and acquired two major road junctions. Still, there are some surprising survivals.

The two small buildings to the right across the lanes of traffic, stranded between the river and the piazza under a huddle of umbrella pines and in a remarkably good state of preservation, are both **Republican temples**. The circular one is commonly known as the **Temple of Vesta** (from its shape rather than from any specific history), though it may well have been dedicated to Hercules, and the rectangular one, though popularly known as the Temple of Manly Fortune, is now (more prosaically but more accurately) thought to be dedicated to Portunus, the harbour and river god.

Across the road, away from the Tiber, is the church of **S. Maria in Cosmedin**. An old church on an even older site, it is famous for a grotesque stone face set in its porch. This carving, the **Bocca della Verità**, the Mouth of Truth, is another image that is much replicated on keyrings, coffee mugs and T-shirts. The gaping mouth has acquired its own myths. The popular myth is that it clamps shut on the hand of a liar, and for this acuity of perception it has been much used to test sexual fidelity. The Bocca's reidentification as a sewer lid added a certain amusement for those who believed themselves to be in the know. Scholars now say that it was a fountainhead, a representation of a bearded river god, which somehow brings it closer to its function as a dispenser of wisdom. Go to any railway station and place a coin rather than a finger in the slot of a plastic replica Bocca della Verità and it will reciprocate far more vigorously and less discreetly than the real thing by spewing out a personalized printed assessment of love, wealth, health, and fortune. Not in Latin, but in Italian – or, indeed, in English: the Bocca della Verità is now a Euro-franchise, slowly retracing the northward march of the Roman Empire, having been spotted at least as far north as Clackett Lane services on the M25. Meanwhile the original remains, a confidently pagan image, as the dominant feature of this Christian church.

Beyond the piazza is a crossing heavy with traffic. Cross here – the follow-the-nun technique is the method of choice here – and then go left along the Via del Circo Massimo, which runs along one side of Rome's once-great stadium, the **Circus Maximus**. It provides a fine view of the Palatine but is otherwise a slightly desolate open space: a long stretch of dusty earth and sparse coarse grass, edged with trees. When police recently cornered and shot dead one of Italy's most violent and wanted criminals on this spot, it seemed a somehow appropriate location.

One of the biggest unions, CGIL, duly organized a protest – against both the repeal of Article 18 and against terrorism – in Rome. Two million turned out. Red flags made the Circo Massimo, site of the Roman chariot races, look like an ocean full of masts and sails. The flags bobbed up and down in the sun, billowing and then going slack. The city even sounded like a marina: that sound of cloth twisting and clapping in the wind.

Tobias Jones The Dark Heart of Italy (2003)

●

A short distance along the road to the right is a statue standing in a small piazza, the Piazzale Ugo La Malfa. This is the entrance to **Rome's Rose Garden** (*il Roseto di Roma*) a genteel and fertile contrast to the arid Circus Maximus. On a gentle slope of the Aventine, it celebrates Rome's long relationship with roses, represented in emblems and paintings, used in ointments and perfumes and of course in gardens for century after century. Roses of every colour, type and fragrance grow here, and although different varieties bloom throughout a long season May and June are probably the high-point months, when the gardens can be smelled long before they are seen. The visitor can simply amble at pleasure along avenues and past thematic exhibitions, but there are also talks from rose experts and art historians, demonstrations of gardening, flower arranging and even cooking with flowers, as well as the stalls of herbalists, florists and organic-food specialists. The guides on the Garden's evening walks discuss (currently only in Italian) the image of the rose from Botticelli to Shakespeare, and a restaurant and a terrace make the best of the view. It could be England but for the brutal mass of the Palatine structures rising across the valley. Yet, as on almost any site in Rome, the earth holds history. From 1645 to the 1930s this was a **Jewish Cemetery**. The remains were removed to the Campo Verano in 1934. After the war the Jewish community gave permission for the Rose Garden to be planted here. In memory of its past, a star of David is mounted on the gate and the pattern of paths follows the shape of a menorah.

To the right-hand side facing the piazzale take the Via di Valle Murcia, which becomes the Via di S. Sabina and climbs steeply up the slope of the **Aventine**. This was a popular spot for the villas and gardens of rich imperial Romans and later with rich medieval Romans. It is popular again now. Climbing the street here between high walls, the smell of jasmine and honeysuckle hints at hidden gardens. The street soon comes into **Parco Savello** on the right. The small park is shaded by orange trees whose blossom, in spring, makes the whole park fragrant and where surprisingly large fruit is borne on small trees in summer. The park is a favourite with mothers and

Church of S. Sabina

small children and with respectable old ladies dressed in navy and grey who walk arm in arm along the gravel paths. There is another of Rome's fine views from the terrace, looking north-west over the Tiber into Trastevere, once again with Rome's familiar landscapes enriching the horizon.

The Aventine is a place of churches. Not the elaborate, marbled, gilded homage of the baroque, but churches of great size, relatively unadorned and dating back to the foundations of faith. This piazza is dominated by the uncluttered lines of **S. Sabina**, the best of them all, a very fine Early Christian basilica built of small reused bricks. Inside its effects are created in simplicity: light and space, white Corinthian columns and high fretted windows glazed with mica. In fact its present appearance is a result of restoration in the nineteenth and twentieth centuries when its subsequent accretions were removed to return it to an appearance as close as possible to its original state. On certain feast days the plainness of its peaceful interior is a contrast to the richness of later ceremonial as cardinals in red, altar boys in lace and monks in white conduct a ritual that has taken place on this spot for 1,600 years. Even the doors, carved in cypress wood, date from the fifth century.

A little way beyond S. Sabina is another early church, **SS. Bonifacio e Alessio**. It is less dramatically beautiful than S. Sabina, having been altered several times over the centuries, but has one extraordinarily elaborate memorial which portrays one of its patron saints and incorporates the (supposed) very staircase under which he died, having returned unrecognized from a sojourn abroad and settled as a servant in his family home.

The **Piazza dei Cavalieri di Malta** at the end of this quiet street is an abrupt change of style and mood. It is quite unlike anything else in Rome. The only piazza designed by Piranesi, it was laid out in 1765, at the same time as the Church of the

Priory of the Knights of Malta, which can only rarely be visited. The piazza, surrounded by walls and buildings secured from the public eye and protected by security cameras, is strange in an appropriately Piranesian way. It is, for a start, a dead end; the road hardly enters it before it veers off down the far side of the hill, and it is usually empty apart from an idling police car. Two sides are surrounded by stone obelisks and stone tablets with relief carvings of pan pipes, severed heads, quivers, a gorgon's-head cornucopia and Maltese crosses. Behind them, dark cypresses and pine trees.

St Peter's Basilica, through the keyhole of the Priory of the Knights of Malta

Those who trek up here do so mainly to see another of Rome's famous views. This one has a certain charm; a trick that pleases however many times you try it. By pressing one eye to the keyhole in the locked gate of the priory (it is obvious from the well-worn panel on the door where hundreds of thousands of hands have braced those peering through) St Peter's dome, two miles distant, rises up in foreshortened perspective, perfectly framed at the end of an avenue of high trees. This is no piece of serendipity but another visual game by Piranesi. Above the door an Egyptian cartouche, a swan's head, a serpent, horns, military colours, an anchor and a quiver.

Take the only road out of the square, the Via di Porta Lavernale, downhill past another church, **S. Angelo**, on the right. Among the large houses on this side of the Aventine are two or three hotels, set in gardens, their location ideal for those prepared to find peace by staying just outside the city centre. The road descends into **Via Marmorata**, one of the main arteries of **Testaccio**. North-west it crosses the Tiber to Porta Portese and Trastevere, south-east it comes to the main-line station at Ostiense.The road acquired its name because this was the route along which the enormous quantities of marble for building passed into the city in antiquity. In places modern excavations have revealed fine marble dust from the working of the material. The nearby port always made this an important place in the economic success of Rome.

Subsequently Testaccio became a traditionally working-class area which has, perhaps inevitably, become fashionable, although it can still feel quite edgy in its more isolated streets by night. The workshops endure, with car-repair garages side by side with artists' studios. The doors of the abattoir (*mattatoio*) may have closed, though a superb carving of a pair of horns survives over premises in Via di Monte Testaccio, but the restaurants which gained their reputations through the quality of their meat, especially offal, have continued to flourish. Testaccio is good for food in general. *Volpetti* at Via Marmorata 47 is famous city-wide for its cheeses and they fill the window: cylinders and slabs in every colour from cream to waxy brown, like so many blocks of masonry, and stamped with their origin. But *Volpetti* is far more than this; it is an old-fashioned and comprehensive delicatessen, its white-coated assistants ranked behind the counter. Smoked ham, spices, breads, vegetables in oil can all be sampled. *Volpetti* is no secret and building on this reputation the owners started *Volpetti Più*, at Via Volta 8, around the corner. This has good basic snack food, including pizza, served from 10 a.m. to 10 p.m., but is best for a light lunch. Alternatively, turn right out of Via Volta into Via Luca della Robbia where *Trattoria*

Butcher, Testaccio covered markets

da Bucatino at number 84 has the cliché Italian-restaurant interior, with checked tablecloths, dusty Chianti bottles and swags of dried garlic. The food is more exciting and better value for money than this might indicate: a good antipasto buffet is certainly enough for lunch and the puddings are worth the detour.

The street runs alongside the eastern edge of Piazza Testaccio and the extensive **covered markets**. Here restaurateurs, traders and nuns buying provisions for their convents shop at dawn, and local Romans thereafter. Meat still lords it here – the butchers' stalls are garnished with bull horns and proud photographs of cows that have become beef – but there are also fish stalls, cheese stalls, bread stalls, wide and garish displays of vegetables next to the saccharine pinks and lavenders of artificial flowers. Older men doggedly peel and chop vegetables to sell ready-prepared, and women sit within small fortifications of boxes and boxes of household cleaning products or piles of cheap shoes. By nine in the morning the customers are mostly housewives, apparently oblivious to the stallholders

Pyramid of Cestius

still bellowing out their wares. The smell of the market is sweet and ripe. Numerous little cafés follow the edge of the square where shoppers can retreat for espresso and *cornetti*, while a couple of streets to the north at Via Giovanni Branca 98 is *Augustorello*, a well-established restaurant serving traditional Roman food, from oxtail to artichokes.

Return to Via Marmorata and turn right past the fire station. The tip of a pyramid is an unmistakable landmark behind the trees. This is the tomb of a first-century BCE Roman Tribune, **Gaius Cestius**. Little is known of Cestius beyond his name. But his tomb – equal in its dramatic impact to the mausoleum of Hadrian and in a far better state of preservation than that of Gaius's own emperor, Augustus – lies just outside the city walls, a long stretch of which including the **Porta S. Paolo** still stands at this point. He is a man whose monument has outlived his language.

I can recall no word
Of anything he did;
For me he is a man who died and was interred
To leave a pyramid.

Thomas Hardy *At the Pyramid of Cestius*
near the Graves of Shelley and Keats

Two millennia later the more recent foreign dead are nestled behind him in a crook of the hefty Aurelian city walls. Turn right at Via Caio Cestio and what is popularly known as the **Protestant Cemetery**, but is more correctly described as the Cemetery of non-Catholics, is on the left. *Resurrecturis* is engraved over the gate. Ring the bell to enter.

The cemetery is the epitome of the secret garden: a hidden, shady place of gravel walks and peace on this hot, noisy intersection. Cats sleep on urns and under marble-feathered angel wings and the few visitors walk quietly. But the very existence of the cemetery was the result of a hard-fought battle between the Roman Catholic church and the families of deceased expatriate Protestants. The present sanctuary, overhung with pines and cypresses and

Monument to his wife by sculptor William Storey (Protestant Cemetery)

Tomb of Devereux Plantagenet Cockburn (Protestant Cemetery)

appealingly maintained in a controlled tangle of jasmine, roses, plumbago and oleander, was originally a wasteland known locally as *fosse dei cani*, the dogs' grave. Burials were undertaken by night for fear of upsetting local religious sensibilities and inscriptions implying any salvation for the non-Catholic were strictly forbidden. Even the use of the phrase *God is love* was rejected by a papal commission. In Italy God's love could only be claimed by Roman Catholics until the late nineteenth century.

The first known interment was of an Oxford scholar, George Langton, who died in 1738 at the age of twenty-five and was buried at the foot of the pyramid. But it was the burial of Keats in 1821, and then of Shelley after he drowned off Livorno two years later, that turned the cemetery itself into a shrine to Romanticism. It became such an idealized burial ground that

Goethe drew a sketch of his own grave in it, though he was eventually to be buried in Germany (although his infant son is interred here). Many of the graves here are of the very young. Rome was not necessarily healthy or safe and for the less hardy or less fortunate the Grand Tour could turn out to be a one-way journey: *infelix pater* – unhappy father – is a lament echoed on many of the gravestones. Expiring in exile, the dead reclaimed their roots: headstones read *'Of Rutland'*, *'Of Alresford in the County of Hampshire'*, *'Of St John's College, Oxford'*, *'Of County Armagh'*. They lie under memorials where neoclassical reliefs stand side by side with weeping seraphim and asphodels with armorial bearings, where Homer's words are inscribed next to St Matthew's and Latin aphorisms alternate with quotations from Shakespeare. In this corner of Rome life-sized stone Victorians recline in the perpetual shade.

Tomb of Rosa Bathurst, Protestant Cemetery

Only a hundred yards further west, across the Via Zabaglia, at the foot of Monte Testaccio, is another cemetery that also holds the remains of young British exiles. **The 1939–1945 British Military Cemetery** contains the 486 graves of those killed in or near Rome while securing the liberation of the city. Here are members of regiments with their own long histories: the Seaforth Highlanders, the London Irish Rifles, the Duke of Wellington's Regiment, the 'Ox. and Bucks' Light Infantry, Queen Victoria's Madras Miners. There are just three

The British Military Cemetery, Monte Testaccio

unidentified soldiers and one airman. There is a doctor, well into middle age, and a young female physiotherapist: '*Kind, kind was she.*' They are not buried in earth wrested from reluctant papal authorities but in ground donated by the Italian people. 'Thank you for freedom' reads one comment in Italian in the visitors' book on the sixtieth anniversary of the liberation.

Here there is an absolute equality in death. In the Protestant Cemetery, after the 1821 sinking of HMS *Naiad* in the mouth of the Tiber, the crew were buried at the captain's expense in a communal grave. However, a young officer, Midshipman Charles Dudley Ryder, the son of the Bishop of Lichfield, has a large monumental grave of his own. In the Military Cemetery the crews of bombers or minesweepers are interred together in groups, whatever their respective ranks.

There is one particularly moving memorial here. On a central plinth a piece of reddish stone is embedded in mortar.

An inscription reads: *This stone from Hadrian's Wall, the northernmost boundary of the Roman Empire, was placed here at the wish of the citizens of Carlisle, England, to commemorate those servicemen from Cumbria who died in the Second World War.*

The hill of **Monte Testaccio** is a man-made one. In antiquity the area was full of warehouses and for nearly half a millennium rubbish – mostly broken pots – was discarded in a heap. In time, covered with the grass of centuries, the rubbish dump became a 118-foot-high hill. It is slightly scruffy by day, very quiet and empty, with just some trees, wild flowers and rather temporary-looking restaurants and clubs dug into its side. It is occasionally open. Enter by the gate in the link fence and climb the steep path to the top and the view; astonishingly, the occasional sliver of broken amphora still protrudes from the ground. By night this is a very different place: its music, its food and its grittier nightlife draw visitors from all over the city.

The old abattoir once stood opposite the renowned restaurant *Checchino dal 1887* at Via di Monte Testaccio 47; they started business at the same time. Diners travel a long way to eat the offal that is the speciality here, although there are many other choices. Spinal cord, intestines and testicles, the stuff of uneasy English merriment, arrives beautifully cooked, far more subtle than hearty. The wine cellar is as good as any in town and the range of cheese is exceptional. It is not cheap and not unknown but it *is* very special.

One of the most amiable Testaccio institutions is *Perilli* at Via Marmorata 39. Come here to relish an ambience, an interior and a style of cooking virtually unchanged over a century and service that is both professional and caring. The vegetables are particularly good but there is first-rate pasta with traditional sauces beautifully cooked, and offal for the connoisseur. Testaccio is still, as it always has been, a point for leaving or entering Rome, with a main-line station, Ostiense, as well as the Metro station, Pyramide. It also has numerous buses and trams heading back into the centre.

WALK 7

The Lateran

- The Celian Hill
- The Churches of S. Clemente, SS. Quattro Coronati,
  S. Stefano Rotondo
- Arch of Dolabella
- S. Giovanni in Laterano
- S. Prassede and S. Croce in Gerusalemme
- The gates of Porta Asinaria and Porto S. Giovanni
- The Amphiteatrum Castrense
- The Museum of Musical Instruments

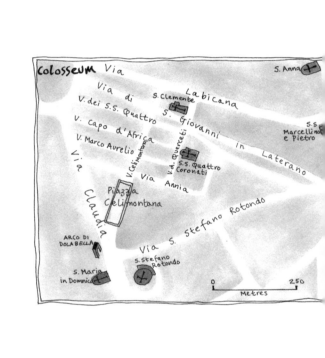

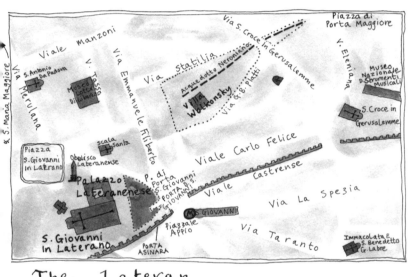

The Lateran

The numbers who congregate around the Colosseum dwindle rapidly if you walk due south onto the **Celian Hill**. Cross over the Via Celio Vibenna (named after an Etruscan hero) and, almost immediately, peace descends. It is a good place for a picnic, overlooking but out of earshot of the Colosseum itself. The ruins of the **Temple of Claudius** are scattered here, along with some isolated historic villas, a fine Renaissance garden and a handful of churches, but mostly it is a place of trees, wild blue geraniums and chicory, dry grass and cicadas. A little train rattles by and then it is quiet again.

However, to the south-east of the Colosseum, the hand of the Roman Catholic church has shaped the streets and the architecture. Up to the fourteenth century the Lateran Palace was the residence of the popes and S. Giovanni in Laterano, the mother church of Rome, was as eminent as St Peter's, drawing the devout into this area and encouraging the glorification of other churches and the growth of religious orders. This is primarily a walk between churches, but churches of such different periods and individual contexts that they provide a template for Rome's history.

The area in the triangle between the Celian Hill, Via di S. Giovanni in Laterano and Via S. Stefano Rotonda mostly comprises residential streets of large, late nineteenth-century houses, built over an area that was once ancient barracks and administrative buildings. Surprisingly little of this is visible today, although there are links with antiquity in or around most of the churches. The area has

Roman suitor

become quite fashionable in recent years, fuelling a growth in small hotels, chic restaurants and a young and energetic sense of community. At the top of many side roads looms the bulk of the fortified SS. Quattro Coronati. From the south-eastern side of the Colosseum, cross over the road and head up Via Capo d' Africa. The *Hotel Capo d'Africa* occupies a rather grand early twentieth-century house. Inside it is stylishly modern and immaculate in interpretation, with large rooms and a lovely roof terrace on which breakfast can be served.

Vecchio Roma tearooms

The increasing number of fashionable wine bars is only equalled by that of tearooms; tea is the drink for those Romans honing radical tastes. *La Mosca Bianca* in Via Ostilla, the street which joins Via Capo d'Africa with Via dei SS. Quattro Coronati, provides both wine and tea as well as cold dishes: cheeses and cured meats are available and coffee is made in an antique machine. Via dei SS. Quattro Coronati has a small and reasonably inexpensive hotel, the *Celio*, in a cream-painted town house with a roof terrace and, a rarity, parking. *Café Café* in the same road, at 44, its yellow-and-blue-painted tables shaded by awnings, has a slightly amateur feel about it, although it is none the worse for that when one considers the importunate waiters and over-slick service of some restaurants immediately around the Colosseum. It offers Mediterranean rather than simply Italian specialities: chickpea soup, vegetables with Greek yogurt dip, avocado-and-parmesan salad or roast aged pork loin – and sixty different sorts of tea.

●

When I'd looked at it earlier, my guidebook had explained that every Catholic order had to build a mother church in Rome, but that many of these orders had died out and accordingly their houses of worship were overgrown with moss, the portals off the hinge, the disaffected altars now just platforms for mice and cats to scamper across. Baroque Rome of grandiose, insincere volutes and illusionistic ceiling paintings was omnipresent, but I kept constantly coming on bits of ancient Rome – an altar to love, an emperor's pyramid, the Mouth of Truth, yet another triumphal arch. Wedged between were slivers of the Rome I liked, medieval Rome exemplified by my favourite church, I Quattro Coronati.

In the rain I was convinced I could smell rotting bones and that all Rome was a cemetery.

Edmund White *The Farewell Symphony* (1997)

●

The third road to cross Via Capo d'Africa and Via dei SS. Quattro Coronati, as you move away from the Colosseum, is the **Via dei Querceti.** The little shrine – an *edicola* – on the intersection with Via dei SS. Quattro Coronati is more than it looks; the location, a gentle backstreet today, was obviously once a place of great significance. This tiny roofed construction with Virgin and child was probably originally a pagan shrine, transformed by Christian pragmatism in the Middle Ages. But this corner has slightly more colourful associations with maternity. It is related that a Pope John VIII was in a procession near S. Clemente one Easter. Unruly crowds caused the pope's horse to rear up, whereupon the

Christian (formerly pagan) shrine, Via dei Querceti

pope went into premature labour, revealing *her*self not as
John but as Joan. A remarkably unsympathetic crowd then
stoned her to death and she was buried at the spot –
presumably here – where the deception was discovered. This
is why, it is said, a newly elected pope has his genitals felt by
the electing cardinals through a hole in a ceremonial
porphyry chair. Except that this too is probably myth and the
story of the holey porphyry throne may well be far older than
the tale of Pope Joan – who was not the Pope John VIII
(872–82) on the papal lists, though supporters of the story
believe that her false name was erased from the record.
Others see this tale as a delicious satire combining every
element that would be most abhorrent to Roman Catholics.
A promiscuous prelate, a woman taking power over men (by
deception, of course), and instability at the very heart of the
Church. An inscription on the wall beside the shrine reads:

'The smile of Mary will cheer up this place if the passer-by will greet her with "Ave Maria".'

> I love the priests in their robes of black, red, violet and white, the Latin Mass, the seminarians with fear in their faces, the old prebendaries in stained soutanes and beautiful greasy Monsignore hats with funny red cords round their waists and fear in their faces, the old women kneeling at confessionals with fear in their faces, the poor cracked hands of the beggars in front of the carved and worked portals of the chapels.

Wolfgang Koeppen *Death in Rome* (1954)

Walking left here as you face the shrine, you will come out on Via di S. Giovanni in Laterano. The church of **S. Clemente**, on the far side of the road, is one of the most fascinating buildings in Rome. It offers a vertical view of the long history of the city, from the first century CE to the twentieth – and it also raises some questions about the origins of Christianity. The church seen from the street dates from the early twelfth century. Much of the medieval building survives, including the Cosmatesque mosaic floor. The technique, beautifully developed by the Cosmati brothers, re-used chips of ancient marble. The frescoes date from a century or two later, the great tombs of the cardinals were constructed in the fifteenth century, the present bell tower was added in the seventeenth, and the white stucco decorations a hundred years later. Restoration is ongoing. Yet a visit to S. Clemente can also be a descent through layers of religious belief: beneath the church is a considerably older basilica, dating to the third or fourth century, of which only the north and south walls and a few fragments are visible. Below this, cool and dark, are several rooms of buildings that include a first-century upper-class house and a pagan *mithraeum* – a temple for the worship of the god Mithras. It is by no means the only one known in Rome but it is the most accessible and it still has its stucco decorations on vaulted ceilings, rooms for the ritual feast and its original altar. Mithras was a god who originated in the east and became popular in first-century Rome, particularly with the army. His rites were secret and *mithraea* were often located underground. Mithras's destiny was to redeem mankind through sacrifice and the religion had a *pater*, or father, at its head and included rituals in which believers were plunged into pools of water. The Irish Dominicans who own the complex today are, however, vigorous in their denial of any similarity whatsoever between the Mithraic cult and Christianity.

Turn back across the road and climb up the steep Via dei SS. Quattro Coronati for a short while before turning right into the forecourt of the church and convent. The sense of a forbidding presence when seen from the streets below is dispersed when this lovely old church is entered from the front where, despite its size and the fact that it was fortified in order to protect the nearby Lateran Palace, a place of peace and light that feels almost forgotten is revealed. The thirteenth-century cloister garden, in particular, is a haven often lit by sun: it is full of greenery and fragments of an earlier church that once stood on the site, and while here it is possible to believe oneself deep in the Italian countryside. There are unique frescoes showing the conversion of the Emperor Constantine in the **Chapel of S. Sylvester**.

To find a church with a very different atmosphere, turn right on leaving and walk into Via Annia, then left into Via Celimontana. This brings you back to the edge of the

Ancient Roman fragment, Piazza di S. Giovanni in Laterano

parkland of the Celio and there, in the middle of the road, is an ancient Roman arch, the **Arco di Dolabella**, erected in the first century and used by Nero as an aqueduct. Take the next turning on the left, into the Via S. Stefano Rotondo, and the church of the same name is on the left. Built right on the crest of the Celian Hill, more than 600 years earlier than the current churches of S. Clemente or SS. Quattro Coronati, it also reflects a very different religious sensibility. This unique church stands quietly under the trees in a location that has always been a little out of the way and was once a place of vineyards. The composer Palestrina lived in a house in these peaceful surroundings. **S. Stefano Rotondo** is one of the earliest Christian churches in Rome, built on top of what was a barracks for foreign legionaries in antiquity. Its circular shape is more eastern than western and is formed around the four equal arms of a Greek cross. To modern tastes the frescoes inside, added in the sixteenth century and depicting in explicit detail the gruesome deaths of martyrs, are either compelling or repellent. The Marquis de Sade, at his more fastidious, found them distasteful. At the same time as the fresco painters were setting to work, Palestrina, informed by similar religious beliefs, wrote a Mass of such unearthly beauty and purity, dedicated to the dead young Pope Marcellus, that the reigning pope rescinded his ban on polyphonic music.

But St Stefano Rotondo, a damp, mildewed vault of an old church in the outskirts of Rome, will always struggle uppermost in my mind, by reason of the hideous paintings with which its walls are covered. These represent the martyrdoms of saints and early Christians; and such a panorama of horror and butchery no man could imagine in his sleep, though he were to eat a whole pig raw, for supper. Grey-bearded men being boiled, fried, grilled, crimped, singed, eaten by wild beasts, worried by dogs, buried alive, torn asunder by horses, chopped up small with hatchets: women having their breasts torn with iron pinchers, their tongues cut out, their ears screwed off, their jaws broken, their bodies stretched upon the rack, or skinned upon the stake, or crackled up and melted in the fire: these are among the mildest subjects. So insisted on, and laboured at, besides, that every sufferer gives you the same occasion for wonder as poor old Duncan awoke, in Lady Macbeth, when she marvelled at his having so much blood in him.

Charles Dickens
Pictures of Italy

Return to the Via S. Stefano Rotondo and turn right. The street eventually comes into the **Piazza di S. Giovanni in Laterano**, a chaotic, unattractive space that seems more of an opportunity for

Corner of S. Giovanni in Laterano

Constantine, saint and emperor

a traffic jam than a planned piazza; here one of the ancient Egyptian obelisks that create a focal point in other Roman squares simply seems obtrusive. On 24 June, the saint's name day is celebrated with a feast of snails in the piazza.

Perhaps the square has a lack of focus because the front entrance to **S. Giovanni in Laterano** is on the far side. The cathedral of the city, head of all the Roman Catholic churches in the world, and a focal point of Christian travel to Rome, is a vast building, almost too large to absorb as a coherent whole. The sense of religious intimacy found in the smaller churches is absent; but the sense of a spiritual and political powerhouse is overwhelming.

For some this is a part of the religious pilgrimage of a lifetime, for others simply another historic site to tick off. Here are confessionals for Polish, Spanish, French and Italian speakers, here the devout kneel before an illuminated plaster statue of the Virgin and Child, and nuns walk in twos and threes looking up in wonder. Other tourists, less awed but more confused, talk more loudly than you might expect, while beggars, mostly East European refugees, many of them women with babies, sit outside in the loggia, legs outstretched, backs straight against the stonework.

●

The nave, consisting of five aisles is of grand proportions, but has been hideously modernized under Borromini, who has enclosed all its ancient columns, except for two near the tribune, in tawdry plaster piers, in front of which are huge statues of the apostles; the roof is gilt and gaudy, the tabernacle ugly and ill-proportioned – only the ancient pavement of opus-alexandrium is fine.

Augustus Hare *Walks in Rome* (1872)

In the cloister, a smaller world is more accessible and in a small, plain room off it are the relics of those in the process of beatification. A worn fragment of Mother Teresa's veil is one of them and links the present with the long and sometimes lurid history of martyrdoms, sanctity, relics and miracles. For one euro a machine dispenses a cigarette-card-size colour picture from a choice of more modern saints. Padre Pio, he of the miraculous *stigmata*, seems to be a favourite.

The Church has not always been as richly endowed, smoothly controlled and (relatively) virtuous as it is today. In 897, at a time of chaos and bloodshed even within the highest echelons of the organization, one of the strangest episodes in ecclesiastical history – an event known as the Cadaver Synod or *synod horrenda* – took place. This was the trial of Pope Formosus by Pope Stephen VII. Pope Formosus, who had died nine months earlier, was disinterred from his tomb in St Peter's and

The Cloister of S. Giovanni in Laterano

Shrine to Padre Pio

cross-questioned on counts of perjury, coveting the papacy and violating canon law. The decomposing and increasingly malodorous Formosus was defended by a co-opted junior deacon, so awed at his task that he could not help giggling nervously. Found guilty, what remained of Formosus was stripped of his papal vestments, had the fingers formerly used to extend the papal blessing cut off, and was interred in a common grave. This was not enough for the populace, which, inflamed by righteous fervour, dug Formosus up again and – in accordance with the ancient Roman instinct – threw him into the Tiber. After floating downstream for a while, he was fished out by a priest and reburied. But even then, the post-mortem travels of Pope Formosus were not over; soon he was dug up yet again, and re-interred in his original tomb and vestments. And Pope Stephen VII was strangled later that year.

Houses are on the ground, walls are falling, sanctuaries are collapsing, the laws are transgressed. The Lateran lies on the ground and the mother of all churches is roofless, open to the blustering winds and the torrential rain.

Petrarch (during the Jubilee of 1350)

To the south-east of the Lateran, the old ancient walls of the city stretch away. There is the large gateway of S. Giovanni and the much older gate, with its towers, the **Porta Asinaria**. In the sixth century this was the entrance opened by treacherous Roman soldiers who admitted the Goth forces under Totilus into the city – which they proceeded to sack. Beyond it, continuing into the Via Sannio, is a flea market, mostly selling crafts and clothes, new and cheap or second-hand, but with more character than the more famous Porta Portese market in Trastevere **(Walk 8)**.

The Via Merulana leads from S. Giovanni to **S. Maria Maggiore**, another vast church, but just before you reach this great basilica there is the beautiful and atmospheric ninth-century church of **S. Prassede**. Its gorgeous Byzantine mosaics are some of the best anywhere. Coming from a bright, busy Roman day into the vaulted richness of gold and jewel-like

Porta Asinaria

colours and an absolute quietness has an impact unlike any other church. For anyone interested in churches it is arguably S. Prassede, not S. Maria Maggiore, which makes a diversion down Via Merulana essential. The Easter vigil is a superb piece of liturgical drama and one of Christianity's oldest celebrations. As Easter Saturday night moves towards Sunday the congregation stand in silence in the dark to either side of the sixteenth-century flight of steps leading downwards from the atrium to the portico. Each holds a slender candle in a cuff. The celebrants, dressed in purple embroidered vestments, bring a brazier to the foot of the stairs. It burns with a new light, struck from a flint. The priest lights the candle of the nearest member of the congregation to each side and they in turn light their neighbours' candles and so light returns to the church and spreads up the stairs. When all the candles are aflame the people are led back into the body of the church and the celebrant returns, now in white. It is mysterious and moving and feels as old as time.

To miss out S. Prassede and S. Maria Maggiore, take the broad, tree-lined boulevard called Viale Carlo Felice. A small park runs along to the right-hand side, between the road and the old walls. As the street comes into **Piazza S. Croce in Gerusalemme**, another city gate appears on the right. Pass through it and from the other side it is possible to see that this is in fact the remains of a small amphitheatre, known as the **Amphiteatrum Castrense**. Its arches have long been filled in and what is left are simply some tall curves of narrow brick which continue on into another long section of buttressed walls, over which the bell tower of the church of **S. Croce in Gerusalemme** can be seen. As in so many other parts of Rome, despite the walls being no more than vestiges of a long-distant way of life there is still a clear change of mood between the busy city within them and the slower, quieter, streets outside.

To enter S. Croce in Gerusalemme return through the Amphiteatrum Castrense and turn right. The great piazza in front of the church is invariably empty. Few sightseers stray from the beaten track and of the thousands who visit S. Giovanni in Laterano very few make the five-minute walk to S. Croce in Gerusalemme. The atmosphere here could not be more different: the Lateran feels at the centre of the city and the Church of S. Croce in Gerusalemme on the periphery. Which, of course, it is. The passionate purpose of its foundation, to contain relics supposedly bought by St Helena, mother of the Christian convert Emperor Constantine, from Jerusalem to Rome, is challenged by changes in Catholic belief and credulity, not to mention modern scientific methods of dating. Although plenty of great Catholic churches have relics, perhaps at S. Croce in Gerusalemme there are just too many:

1. Three fragments of the True Cross.
2. Fragments of the pillar at which Christ was scourged.
3. The crib in which he was laid and a fragment of his sepulchre.
4. One of the nails from the Cross.
5. The title of the Cross.
6. Two thorns from the Crown of Thorns.
7. The index finger of St Thomas which he placed in Christ's wounds to convince himself of the veracity of His rising from the dead.
8. The title of the cross of the good thief. In an annexe.

The True Cross was said to have moved outside the normal conventions of the material world when it was permeated by Christ's blood. Catholic theology maintained that because of this the Cross could be divided infinitely without ever being diminished in size or power.

St Helena also brought home the sponge used to mop the

crucified Christ's face, some earth from the Holy Land and the staircase from Pontius Pilate's house upon which Jesus was tried. This is held within the church of *Scala Sancta* near the Lateran where many faithful from all over the world and a few schoolchildren urged on by their nuns still climb it torturously, on their knees. It seems that in the late nineteenth century there were numerous other relics accounted for at S. Croce. Many were put away as the veneration of relics declined in importance but the ones still on display should be seen, not least for the ornate ingenuity of the reliquaries that contain them.

●

'The list of relics on the right of the apsis of S. Croce includes, the finger of S. Thomas Apostle . . . one of the pieces of money with which the Jews paid the treachery of Judas; great part of the vail (*sic*) and hair of the most blessed Virgin; a mass of cinders and charcoal in the form of a loaf, with the fat of St Laurence, martyr; one bottle of the most precious blood of our Lord Jesus Christ; another of the milk of the most blessed Virgin; a little piece of the stone where Christ was born; a little piece of the stone where our Lord sat when he pardoned Mary Magdalen; of the stone where our Lord wrote the law, given to Moses on Mount Sinai; of the stone where reposed the saints Peter and Paul; of the cotton which collected the blood of Christ; of the manna which fed the Israelites; of the rod of Aaron which flourished in the desert; of the relics of seven prophets.'

Augustus Hare, quoting 'Percy's Romanism'
in *Walks in Rome* (1871)

●

Ornamental brickwork, S. Agnese Fuori
Le Mura

On the Aventine

The Protestant Cemetery

TEMPLE OF VESPASIAN

S. LUCA E MARTINA

TEMPLE OF SATURN

ARCH OF SEPTIMIUS SEVERUS

CURIA

The Forum

Buddhist monks at the Colosseum

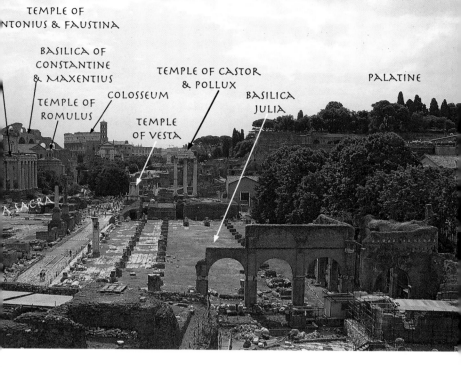

TEMPLE OF
NTONIUS & FAUSTINA

BASILICA OF
CONSTANTINE
& MAXENTIUS

TEMPLE OF CASTOR
& POLLUX

PALATINE

TEMPLE OF
ROMULUS

COLOSSEUM

BASILICA
JULIA

TEMPLE
OF VESTA

A. SACRA

he Colosseum from the Esquiline

Original Roman forest in the Botanic
Gardens

Gammarelli, tailors by appointment to the Pope

The Circus of Maxentius, Via Appia Antica

The church is historically interesting. In ancient times the area was occupied by wealthy Roman families and the remains of their buildings and monuments are still being discovered. S. Croce is embedded in antiquity and various ruins can be seen all around it. The amphitheatre (Castrense) is to one side, and to the other is a large fourth-century hall, known as the **Temple of Venus and Cupid**, and the sixth-century Porta Maggiore which once carried an aqueduct.

Helena's own estates here were built on a palace and gardens established by Heliogabalus, a short-lived young emperor of oriental extraction and sympathies, that covered the area. His memory is notoriously connected with roses: even in this city of imaginatively cruel deaths, suffocation by rose petals, as pictured in Sir Lawrence Alma-Tadema's famous painting *The Roses of Heliogabalus*, seems particularly perverse. Another historic figure whose legend connects with this spot is Pope Sylvester II. A scholar and scientist who collected books and scientific instruments and who improved upon the hydraulic organ, he was believed by ordinary people to be in league with the devil. (Organs seem to have been markers of dubious associations: Nero too had one.) He was said to have been told in a dream that he would die in Jerusalem and in 1003 he supposedly dropped dead while saying Mass at S. Croce in Gerusalemme.

The hall of Helena's palace, known as the **Sessorian**, was used as the foundation for the basilica in the fourth century and it has been amended, restored and partly rebuilt since with a pretty rococo façade. Various chapels, one constructed in what is believed to have been Helena's bedroom, are reached through doors and corridors but a sense of the hybrid architecture and the picturesque setting among ruins is best appreciated from outside.

Within the same large group of ruins, just to the left of the church as you face it, is the **Museum of Musical Instruments**.

Housed in a large and characterless old building, looking out over gardens, this museum is even less visited than S. Croce, which is a shame as it has a huge collection of fine and often unique pieces. The collection has 3,000 instruments. Many are displayed in eighteen halls on the first and second floors. Most famous is the fortepiano by Cristofori, which was a prototype for the modern piano, and a Barberini enharmonic harp, dating back to the early seventeenth century.

Inside, surprisingly for a museum dedicated to the beauty of sound, there is a stifling silence. (Although visitors can in theory switch on recordings of some instruments, they are perhaps deterred by the proportion of visitors to attendants, which is heavily weighted in favour of the latter.) Though not hot inside it is airless. The rooms are dull, with neither the richness of some Roman museums as a backdrop, nor the dazzling modernity of others, and ropes partition off several of the more valuable instruments, which makes them hard to see, much less appreciate. Despite all this it should not be missed by any connoisseur of music. It has a good collection of ancient instruments and ones from Africa and Asia, and there are some fascinating and pretty barrel organs, glass organs, decorated harpsichords and painted music cabinets from the seventeenth and eighteenth centuries. But in some ways the museum feels more like an auctioneers' warehouse: everything perfectly well maintained, some real gems in the collection, but a certain lack of energy. It deserves a better and more central location. Nevertheless, the garden setting comes into its own in summer when concerts are held outside.

The young man on this museum's ticket office and sales desk is preoccupied with his telephone conversation. The tourists slink out and from inside this place of silence the attendant can still be heard, still shouting into his mobile, as the visitor returns to Piazza S. Croce in Gerusalemme.

WALK 8

Trastevere: Three Strolls and a Boat Trip

- The Janiculum
- S. Pietro in Montorio
- Tempietto di Bramante
- Ponte Sisto
- Porto Settimiana
- Villa Farnesina
- Palazzo Corsini
- Botanic Gardens
- S. Maria in Trastevere
- Museum of Trastevere
- Piazza Piscinula
- Churches of S. Cecilia di Trastevere and S. Francesco a Ripa
- Porta Portese Market

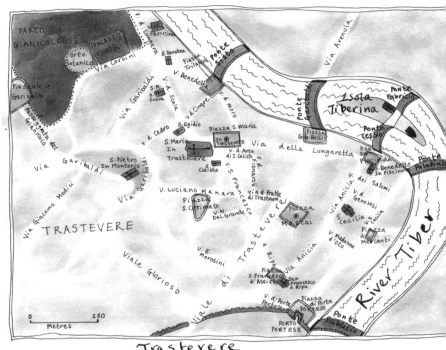

PARCO
GIANICOLENSE

PALAZZO
CORSINI

Orto
Botanico

Piazzale G.
Garibaldi

Passeggiata del
Gianicolo

V. di Lungara

V. Farnesina

V.d. Corsini

Via Corsini

S. Dorotea

Via Garibaldi

S.M.
D. Scala

V. d. Scala

V. Benedetta

Ponte
Trilussa

Ponte Sisto

V. d. Moro

Ponte
Garibaldi

Isola
Tiberina

Ponte
Fabricio

V.d. Cinque

Via Arenula

Piazza S. Maria

V. d. Cedro

S. Egidio

In
Trastevere

Ponte
Cesto

S. Maria
In
Trastevere

Via   della   Lungaretta

Ponte
G. G. Belli

Via Garibaldi

S. Pietro
In Montorio

V. d. Arco
di S. Calisto

Pza.
In Piscinula

Ponte
Palatino

Via Giacomo Medici

Via Garibaldi

S.
Calisto

V. S. Francesco

V. d.
Fienaroli

S. Benedetto
In Piscinula

V. dei Salumi

V. Luciano Manara

Piazza
S. Cosimato

V.N.
Del Grande

V. d. Fratte
di Trastevere

Via   di   Trastevere

Piazza
Mastai

V. d.
Genovesi

V. Anicia

Via Sicilia

Piazza
dei
Mercanti

TRASTEVERE

V. E.
Morosini

V. Madonna
d'Oro

Viale Glorioso

Ripa

Via Anicia

Viale   di   Trastevere

S. Francesco
d'Assisi

San
Francesco
A Ripa

Piazza
di Porta
Portese

V. di Porta
Portese

Ponte
Sublicio

PORTO
PORTESE

River Tiber

0   250
Metres

Trastevere

On the west bank of the Tiber the ancient area of Trastevere can no longer assert that it is the unique face of old Rome, although many guidebooks make this claim on its behalf. The legendary Trasteverian dialect has disappeared, along with the honest artisans and the tough independence of the Trasteverini. (Their proudest claim was never to have crossed the river, their historic reputation was to be inclined to violence.) Their traditions have been replaced by fashionable wine bars, small restaurants and artists' studios. Trastevere, around the broad Piazza S. Maria in Trastevere, is youthful in spirit, ebullient by night and popular with young foreigners who find the rents here cheaper than in the historic centre on the other side of the river, and with academics from the nearby American School at Rome.

However, Trastevere (the name simply means 'across the Tiber', *Tevere* being the Roman name of the river) manages to retain a great deal of charm; its muddle of streets, archways, piazzas, medieval houses and convent churches has changed little over the last few centuries. Once away from the main streets, the washing suspended from balconies, the calling from street to window and the untidily parked old cars could be in the backstreets of any town in southern Italy.

●

You enter into a region of empty, soundless, grass-grown lanes and alleys, where the shabby houses seem mouldering away in disuse and yet your footstep brings figures of startling Roman type to the doorways. There are few monuments here, but no part of Rome seems more historic, in the sense of a ponderous past . . . When the yellow afternoon sunshine slept on the sallow battered walls and lengthened the shadows in the grassy courtyards of small closed churches, the place acquired a strange fascination.

Henry James *Roderick Hudson*

●

Resting street entertainer, Trastevere

By day Trastevere is a sleepy, quiet residential area. A very few keen tourists, a couple of nuns eating ice creams, housewives buying bread. In early evening the northern Europeans and Americans find their pizzas or spaghetti in the more obvious trattorias or pick through the wares of the peddlers – CDs, faux-Prada handbags, teak giraffes and silver jewellery – and explain to unconvinced children why they can't buy a puppy. Finally, late into the night, the little bars buzz, the simple wooden tables of lesser-known restaurants are doing non-stop trade, bargain hunters cluster round the second-hand book stalls in the **Piazza S. Maria in Trastevere** and *gelati* and *granita* kiosks work into the early-morning hours. The fortune-tellers set up their pitches and their dog-eared cards in the Via della Paglia and the audience trickles out of the late show at *Pasquino*, the English-language cinema in Vicolo del Piede. Foreign films have that edge even in Rome.

In the late nineteenth century a broad road – the Viale di Trastevere – was driven through the district and to a degree the two areas to either side of it became quite distinct in character. The north is more popular, with fashionable shops, cafés and clubs; live music, street theatre and stalls are all part of its life after dark.

The southern section is less well known and less flamboyant. It has more of a sense of its own direction, with a large working market in the **Piazza S. Cosimato** by day, sturdy café-bars and a tight network of small streets and medieval piazzas that hide some real delights – not of famous buildings (although one of Trastevere's finest churches lies in this area) but of fragments of construction from the Middle Ages.

The whole district is easily covered in half a day but in many ways it is in an area worth experiencing on shorter visits, at different times of day and, if possible, in different seasons.

STROLL 1: THE JANICULUM

The descent from the Janiculum is particularly enchanting in the evening. Either catch the 870 bus, or take a taxi to Piazza Garibaldi – or, for the more energetic, take the steep walk from Vicolo del Cedro, behind Piazza S. Egidio in Trastevere itself. The statue of Garibaldi is at the top of the hill, but walk a short way on the far side of the crest and there is a wonderfully dramatic **statue of his Brazilian wife**, **Anita**. This delightful bronze is easy to miss, which is a pity, as here she leaps to defend Rome against the French, her hair flowing, her gun brandished above her head in the approved revolutionary style, and clutching her infant to her breast. She died shortly after the action that is depicted.

I received your letter amid the round of cannonade and musketry. It was a terrible battle being fought here from the first to the last light of day. I could see all its progress from my balcony. The Italians fought like lions. It is a truly heroic spirit that animates them. They make a stand here for their honour and rights, with little ground for hope that they can resist, now they are betrayed by France.

Since the 30th April, I go almost daily to the hospitals, and though I have suffered, for I had no idea before how terrible gunshot wounds and wound-fevers are, yet I have taken pleasure, and great pleasure, in being with the men. There is scarcely one who is not moved by a noble spirit. Many, especially among the Lombards, are the flower of Italian youth.

Margaret Fuller to Ralph Waldo Emerson,
10 June 1849

The **Janiculum** is not one of the legendary (if sometimes elusive) seven hills of Rome, but a long, high ridge that runs parallel to the Tiber and affords some magnificent views of the city. To see the same breadth of view but from the east walk up to the Pincio **(Walk 3)**. The **Garibaldi Monument**, with the great man on his horse, looks down over the city near the point of his heroic action at the walls of Rome. At midday each day a cannon is fired from the Janiculum, in his memory. It can be heard throughout the city. A puppet show and a small merry-go-round draw parents and children, elderly couples take an evening promenade, and kiosks selling metallic-looking balloons, cold drinks and snacks give an old-fashioned air to this popular vantage point.

The larger buildings – the ubiquitous Victor Emmanuel II Monument, St Peter's to the left, the domed roof of the Pantheon and the ruins of the Palatine to the far right – are easily identifiable, though the view can be hazy in summer. Perhaps the best time to gaze out over the city is in spring when leaves do not yet block the view, the distant mountains are capped with snow and the clarity of light brings the tiled roofs of Trastevere very close and gives the earthy colours a beautiful clarity.

Two helpful schematic maps which once identified the monuments are now more indicative of other aspects of Rome. The perspex chosen to frame the maps has long clouded and crazed over and not been replaced and, like so much else in Rome, the maps are covered in graffiti, some of it highly specific: 'Tourists, we hate you', for example.

Turn right as you face the city, walk down under the trees and you eventually hit the serpentine bends of Via Garibaldi; follow this and the church of **S. Pietro in Montorio** comes into sight, standing on a bluff and overlooking the city. The view is superb, the church imposing in a bulky way, but it is for the neoclassical **Tempietto** set in the small courtyard that visitors come here. Built by Bramante, on what was then supposed to be the site of St Peter's crucifixion, it is near to perfection.

Continue along Via Garibaldi, taking the steps down to the right which plunge steeply between high walls set with old street lamps. There is something grotto-like and forgotten in the accretions of creepers, moss and fern, the flaking buildings and the organic smell of dampness as you descend; but at the bottom the mood changes abruptly as the Vicolo del Cedro comes straight into the bright heart of Trastevere. A simple *osteria* on a narrow backstreet leading left here affords a quiet opportunity to eat proper Roman food, without the tourist concessions or the associated prices. Salt cod with raisins and pine nuts is one of many specialties. *Da Lucia* is at Vicolo del Mattonato 2.

Cross over the Tiber from the city, via the pedestrian-only **Ponte Sisto**. While Romans have needed to be persuaded of its pedestrian status with the erection of bollards, gates and hefty chains, the commerce of the bridge itself has a rather medieval air. Here street traders sell their wares from sheets spread on the ground, beggars – often, this being Rome, clutching real coffee in a polystyrene coffee-cup – call out for money, musicians play (indeed, in the evening, whole ensembles play) and fortune-tellers read the Tarot or play Chase the Lady. On the far side, crossing the road, you come straight into the little **Piazza Trilussa**. Trilussa (Carlo Alberto Sallustri, 1871–1950) was a popular poet and raconteur who wrote in the Trasteverian dialect. A wonderful statue to one side of this little piazza captures him for ever in mid-anecdote, leaning over a bar, gesticulating with his stone fingers. An overhanging plane tree points up the theme of his poem '*All' Ombra*' – 'To Shade' – inscribed on the plinth.

Monument to dialect poet Trilussa

On Piazza Trilussa itself are several cafés and bars and *Pizza Piazza*, a basic, late-night pizza takeaway that sells delicious slices, herby and running with cheese, sweet with tomatoes. In the angle of Via del Moro and Via Politeama is a small wine bar, *Ferrara*. Drinkers chat on a long bench set against the frontage; inside it opens into two white-washed rooms on different levels, slightly Moorish in feel with their low seats and deep cushions. Service is a bit haphazard – not because of lack of goodwill but because the barman loves his wine and has a superb collection, and gives every guest the benefit of his advice and enthusiasm. Various dishes come and go on the counter: spiced meatballs, hard-boiled eggs, cubes of herby olive-oil bread, spicy pâté. People help themselves; it all seems delightfully unpoliced. In fact, there is a set price for wine – a price which includes these hearty snacks. Stay long enough and you won't need dinner.

Detail of fountain, Piazza Trilussa

On the far side of the piazza is an Indian restaurant set in an abundant and untamed garden behind the fountain. The flavours are as luscious, and as different, as the position. It may be hard to imagine eating Indian dishes in Rome, but *Surya Mahal* uses local food to produce superb northern Indian specialities, widely considered the best Indian food in the city.

From Piazza Trilussa three equally appealing streets fan out. Via del Moro, Via Benedetta and Vicolo dei Cinque are all typical of the area and are worth exploring. In fact, Trastevere is one of the areas of Rome that most rewards casual pottering through its streets. It is a district of collective charm rather than easily inventoried sights. At Via del Moro 39 is a traditional and efficient local post office presided over by a sternly competent *signora*, with one of the best postcard collections in town.

Mannequin, Trastevere

These are shops which serve the local population: there is excellent (even for Rome) fresh pasta at number 32, and an irresistible bread and biscuit shop at number 15.

The English-language bookshop – *The Almost Corner Bookshop*, at number 48 – is a wonderful resource for expatriates. Every day the owner can be found cleaning the small stretch of street outside, removing cigarette ends in this corner of a foreign world. On his crammed shelves are a fine selection of classics, history, art, fiction, philosophy, crime, poetry and every conceivable book on Rome. A best-seller this year has been a calendar of improbably handsome young priests. But the *Almost Corner* provides other services to the longer-term visitor. Here is the place for small ads: numerous flats and studios for rent, language instruction, kittens given away, singing lessons, even a husband-for-hire – which turns out to be simply a matter of carpentry and plumbing.

From Piazza Trilussa take an oblique right turn down the Via Ponte Sisto and into Via S. Dorotea and on to a small crossroads. At number 20, right on the corner, is a famous Trasteverian institution: *Romolo*. This restaurant, with its romantic walled garden, is in the medieval house supposed to have been lived in by Raphael's mistress, La Fornarina. The food is outstanding, though Romolo's can suffer from the problem of all high-profile Roman restaurants: close your eyes and it could be New York, London or Frankfurt behind the gentle guitar music. Ahead is the broad Via Garibaldi, but turning left here you pass through the surprisingly narrow **Porta Settimiana**. It is a picture-book city gate with crenellated ramparts and defensive embrasures. Built by the Emperor Septimius Severus in the late second century, it became part of the third-century Aurelian wall – constructed as Rome came under threat from invaders – which remained the city boundary until the 1600s. Today it is home to numerous pigeons whose half-grown fledglings peer from its many feather-lined arrow slits like figures revealed in an Advent calendar.

A few minutes' walk beyond the gate is the **Villa Farnesina**, standing on the right and next to the river. No longer sitting in its once-glorious river gardens (these were destroyed when the Tiber embankment was erected in the 1870s) it remains a delightful example of a Renaissance villa. Built in 1511, its mellow faded red, ochre and russet exterior still contains some sensual and exuberant frescoes of flowers and the sea, of gods and goddesses, figures from history, animals, marine creatures, stars and angels. Astonishingly, this jewel of a house is never crowded with visitors. It was once the location for the most splendidly extravagant parties given by its first owner, Agostino Chigi ('The Magnificent'), a powerful Sienese banker and patron of the artist Raphael. His flamboyant party piece was throwing all his gold dinnerware into the river as a demonstration of his boundless wealth. (The next day he would retrieve them from the nets that he had laid underwater.) The spot has an even older history: it stands on the site of what some believe to have been Julius Caesar's country estate – the house where he sequestered Cleopatra when he brought her to Rome.

Returning towards the Settimiana gate, take Via Corsini where a huge magnolia tree dominates the whole street. The **Palazzo Corsini**, on the corner with Via della Lungara, was once the home, and salon, of the notorious Swedish queen Cristina, who abdicated her throne when she converted to Catholicism in the mid-seventeenth century. Its exquisite, and unaltered, eighteenth-century library is, sadly, only open to scholars and with prior permission.

Grotto, Botanic Gardens

The gardens of the Palazzo are today the **Botanic Gardens of Rome**. This series of avenues, glades, fountains and baroque follies climbing up the side of the Janiculum Hill is a wonderfully peaceful, hidden place. It is never over-manicured or overtly educational although it can be highly informative. Perhaps the most charming displays are the historic perfumed rose garden (which illustrates the long shared history of roses and the city) and the extensive Physic Garden of medicinal plants. Mostly the gardens are a cool and sensual retreat from the heat and noise of the city. Each turn reveals a surprise: a stream bed running through great boulders, a tree with blooms like cooked lobster claws, a large shady forest of massive bamboo, all verticals and striped and dappled light, an overgrown and picturesquely decaying grotto, and, always, the soft and sometimes unidentifiable fragrances of growing things. Perhaps the best surprise is one of the least overtly spectacular. In the top right-hand corner is a remnant of the last original forest that covered Rome before it *was* Rome. On a grassy hillside are large evergreen and deciduous oaks, field maples, hornbeam and buckthorn, with acanthus and iris growing beneath the trees. It is an uncultivated and abundant ancient woodland: living, thriving history.

Walk on up the path and within minutes there is a fine view (slightly obscured by foliage in summer) of what is, by comparison, modern Rome. The familiar domes and distant hills, the chariot on the Victor Emmanuel II Monument, seem quite close but you still have to strain to hear the distant roar of civilization. The gardens have a gate giving straight onto the summit of the hill; regrettably, it seems to be permanently shut these days. Open, it would allow visitors to enjoy the Janiculum, wander onto the Via Garibaldi and down into Trastevere: a lovely circuit for a walk.

But, for now, there is no alternative but to leave the gardens the way you came. Turn right at the end of Via Corsini and you pass again under the Porto Settimiana. Follow Via della Scala, another of Trastevere's appealingly lively streets, with its architecture still harking back to when Trastevere was really just a village. Stop at the pharmacy next to the church of **S. Maria della Scala**. It is not quite what it appears to be. It is, for a start, nearly 500 years old and throughout its history has been run by monks. Where the monks once brewed herbal panaceas for everything from worms to agues or the plague, the modern shop now sells the usual remedies for sunburn, hangovers and indigestion and dispenses prescriptions. But upstairs the old pharmacy has been kept intact and is a curiosity well worth a visit.

Via della Scala comes into Piazza S. Egidio where the small **Museo di Trastevere** offers an appealing look at the history of this part of Rome. Little Classical or Renaissance glory here but, instead, the bustle and intrigue of trade and craft and survival, from the Middle Ages to the nineteenth century. Prints and artefacts follow the great families, the merchants, the Jewish community, the Church and the native Trasteverini through the centuries. Go in, if only briefly, to see Rome as it was at the height of the Grand Tour: the Rome that Boswell, Keats and Shelley, Dickens, James and Hawthorne all knew. From this tiny piazza there is the option of a climb from the Vicolo del Cedro, to the right, which eventually comes to the top of the Janiculum.

Via della Scala ends at a right angle to the side of one of Rome's most famous churches. But just before the piazza is *La Tana di Noantri*, a reliable *osteria*, hardly unknown to tourists but good for lunch, in a pretty and protected position in a tiny walled square. It has all the staples and amiable middle-aged waiters. There are very few hotels in Trastevere but one lovely one lies up Vicolo del Piede, the next street left. *Hotel Santa Maria* was converted from a sixteenth-century convent and its rooms lie around a courtyard garden, behind high gates. There is even parking here, a great rarity in Rome. But continue on and you come out into **Piazza S. Maria in Trastevere**, a handsome square dominated by the **Basilica and Romanesque tower of S. Maria**. Its striking medieval façade has a rich gold mosaic in Byzantine style and a frieze of ecclesiastical statues which almost seem to dance to some invisible music. The interior has further lovely mosaics, particularly in the apse, some columns dating from antiquity, an early-seventeenth-century gilded wooden roof (by Domenichino) and a delicate multicoloured Cosmatesque marble floor. In front of the church, the steps of the large fountain are a resting place for the weary who rest beneath the shady overhang of its vast stone shells.

The cafés and restaurants around the piazza have become increasingly fashionable and expensive in the last few years, though *Galeassi*, in a pretty pink and grey house, on the corner with Vicolo del Piede, has been in business since 1907 and is still surprisingly traditional, given its outlook onto Trastevere's most fashionable view and its sunny location. Here you can have carpaccio of swordfish, home-made gnocchi, or veal and lemon with real flavour despite the delicacy of its ingredients. The painstaking waiters have no English – but then, most of their customers are Italian.

Whichever café you sit outside none of the waiters will hurry you as you linger over a single espresso or ice cream,

S. Maria in Trastevere

and the location is wonderful for watching everybody else and feeling Roman. At *Caffè delle Arance* – where fresh orange juice is the refreshing speciality and a Bellini or Mimosa a sensual, if exorbitant, luxury – patrons sit surrounded by small trees, shady awnings and cheerful mountains of oranges.

On the far south-east corner of the square a relief sculpture commemorates the Second World War resistance fighters who opposed the German occupation of 1943–4. Three hundred and thirty-five men, including resistance members and randomly selected civilians, were shot in the Ardeatine Caves in reprisal for a resistance bomb attack **(Walk 10)**. Among them were a priest, a 72-year-old man and 15-year-old boy.

On the nearby corner is one of Rome's many witty small

Fountain in Via della Cisterna

drinking fountains: a stack of stone barrels. A pretty route here is to go down either the Via Arco di S. Calisto or the parallel street, Via della Cisterna, and on reaching the bottom turn right into Via dei Fienaroli. Via dei Fienaroli is a quiet, narrow street with houses covered in creepers but some of Trastevere's nicest shops and restaurants are here. *Bibli* at number 28 is much more than the bookshop that its name implies. Through the door the space unravels into shelves of books (few of them in English), a little restaurant, an Internet café and an art gallery. Concerts are held here: classical music and jazz, poetry recitals and lectures. At Via dei Fienaroli 12 is a small and mellow club, *Selarum*, where an evening's relaxation can be had, listening to live jazz and drinking cocktails in a sweet-smelling garden surrounded by tangled creepers. Or, if serious food is what you are after, *Al Fienaroli* is more generally Mediterranean in flavour than strictly Italian and has a good choice for vegetarians. It is bright, with an edge of minimalist chic, energetic and keen to please. It is the antithesis of the traditional trattoria.

The mood changes if you go through the Piazza S. Calisto and follow the Via S. Cosimato into the large and more workaday Piazza di S. Cosimato. Here there is a large local market and several excellent restaurants. Two of the best specialize in fish: *Alberto Ciarla*, at Piazza di S. Cosimato 40, has old-fashioned service, a superbly imaginative menu, and an international reputation and *Capo de Fero*, at Via S. Cosimato 15, is also first-class and very good on pasta and cheese. From here the Via Natale del Grande leads into Via di S. Francesco a Ripa which crosses the Viale di Trastevere.

STROLL 3: SOUTHERN TRASTEVERE

The southern side of Trastevere simply continues on from the northern part of the district, but for a sense of its relationship with the rest of Rome it can also be approached across the river via **Tiber Island**. **Ponte Cestio** is the ancient bridge which joins the

Ponte Rotto, seen through Ponte Cestio

island with the western bank of the river at Lungotevere Anguillara. Cross the road and descend a small flight of steps to the left and past a medieval palazzo, **Palazzo Mattei** (one of many owned by this once-powerful and brutal family), which stands to one side of the very attractive **Piazza in Piscinula**, the location of a fish market in the Middle Ages and which possibly covers the remains of Ancient Roman baths. Good fish continues to be sold here; *La Cornucopia*, a friendly, slightly smarter than average trattoria with excellent and knowledgeable service, has a fine selection, and there are two good pizza restaurants.

The little church of **S. Benedetto**, the smallest Romanesque church in the city and the one with the oldest bell, hides in the corner. A seventeenth-century façade conceals an interesting eleventh-century interior, which can only be seen by ringing the bell on the door to the right as you face the church.

The narrow and enclosed lanes which lead off Piazza in Piscinula are worth exploring, especially by night when tiny restaurants seem to spring from nowhere: a few tables with paper tablecloths, chairs under a vine, house wine and simple food. The low lighting preserves the timeless atmosphere. Once-grand houses have come down in the world but have lost none of their charm, the streets here are less cluttered and frenetic than further north, alleyways disappear mysteriously under arches. It is not an area of hotels – that is part of its appeal – but it is possible to stay here at a quite elegant bed and breakfast, at *Domus Tiberina* at Via in Piscinula 37.

Leave the piazza on the far right-hand side and pass through one of the dark archways as you walk up **Via dell' Arco dei Tolomei**. Turn left into Via dei Salumi and right into Vicolo di Atleta, a tiny street of great character and not over-restored – its old houses are decorated with fragments of even more ancient carvings. It takes its name from the antique marble statue of an athlete wielding a strigil which was excavated here, a statue now, like so much else, in the Vatican Museums (**Walk 9**). Turn left into Via dei Genovesi and then right into Via S. Cecilia to come out in front of **Santa Cecilia in Trastevere**. This airy, restrained church is dedicated to the patron saint of music, whose eventual martyrdom, after a gruesome and unsuccessful attempt at execution by suffocation in the steam of a Roman bath, supposedly took place on this spot. She was disinterred in the late sixteenth century and her body, still with the wounds that eventually killed her showing on her neck, remained whole. A painted statue was made of her as she was found and lies before the altar (a copy is in Albi cathedral in France).

To request her protection during a concert performance, or for a musical examination, the petitioner must write the name of the saint on a white ribbon and his or her own name on a yellow ribbon. The two ribbons must then be tied to a green candle in which the petitioner must secure two laurel leaves. When the musician succeeds in his or her task, the ribbons and the candle must be buried in a big plant-pot filled with pink flowers or in a garden. Ashes from the burned laurels are to be kept in a small wooden box. If the aid of Saint Cecilia is requested several times, it is advisable to collect all the ashes from the burned leaves in the same box.

'Ritual' from *Rome: A Guide to the Eternal City* (1999)

The remains of ancient baths were subsequently found under the church. Also underneath the church are the remains of a house that may have belonged to the saint's family. The church, though not exceptional, is large and pleasing and has a garden in front of it. A nun in a wimple and wielding a book of accounts has rather stern custody of the excavations, which may be visited all day for a small charge. On Tuesday and Thursday mornings it is also possible to visit the convent attached to the church. This more than repays the effort of a return visit if necessary and of facing the evident resentment of the presiding nun at importunate – if financially useful – visitors who wish to do this. The peaceful convent has a nuns' choir from which the body of the church below can be viewed through fretted screens and which contains the unique and wonderful **frescoes of the Last Judgement** by Cavallini, in which magnificent bejewelled angels have gold, red and pink feathered wings. Despite their freshness and energy, the frescoes are nearly 800 years old. The nun will leave you in no doubt that a further donation is expected at this point.

Leaving the forecourt of S. Cecilia and crossing the road, a small square with several houses dating from the Middle Ages lies straight ahead. **Piazza Mercanti** once stood by the Ripa Grande, a bustling port on the Tiber, where merchants and their wares – marble, granite, spices, wine and food – filled the street with noise, muddle and business. Today it is a rather carefully restored piazza of flowery balconies with a stylish *osteria*. It is worth walking out on the right-hand side as you face the river and pausing for a moment at the intersection with the Via d. Porto. From here, looking south-east, is a fine view of the hilly Aventine.

Turn right beyond the Via d. Porto, right again into the Via Madonna d'Orto and left into Via Anicia which passes the sleepy forecourt of **S. Francesco a Ripa**. In this rather

Hat stall, Porta Portese market

improbable location is the Altieri chapel which contains Bernini's sculpture of the **Ecstasy of Blessed Ludovica Albertoni**. The draped Ludovica writhes, her head thrown back, her hands clutching her breasts as they are pierced by grace. Like the *Ecstasy of St Teresa*, also by Bernini and in the church of **S. Maria della Vittoria**, it is a work of brilliance which observers can find discomfiting, so closely – to the modern gaze, at least – are the spiritual and the erotic combined. Continue for a short distance further, turn left and you come to another section of the walls of Rome. Ahead lies the gate of the **Porta Portese** and, on Sundays, one of Rome's most famous flea markets.

It is not quite what it was. Until recently its origins in the post-war black market and its eclectic mixture of junk – from military binoculars to old furniture, books, kitsch, and the occasional genuine antique – made it an exciting, slightly edgy place to explore. It is increasingly just a matter of red,

Porta Portese

blue and yellow nylon football strip, cheap shoes, cheap fake
sunglasses and cheap pirated CDs; it could be any large
market in any country. It is heavily policed, extremely
crowded and goes on for ever between the rather bleak blocks
of housing that characterize the area. But there are still
occasional echoes of the past. Nuns haggle hard over bright
beach towels with scenes of tropical sunsets, a boy dodges
through the dense crowd with a tray full of espressos at
shoulder level, a man on the second corner sells pets: a rather
inert metallic-blue blackbird is just too high up to check for
paint, some dormice look unnervingly tasty and gaudy parrots
shriek and bite. English passers-by look appalled. Teenage
boys surround a stall selling fishing rods and tackle and up
one of the side streets a strange mixture of 1920s French
pornographic photos and soft pink pictures of sleepy saints
wreathed in celestial flowers vie for space on the vendor's
rickety card table.

Nearby, a man walks swiftly from one parked motorbike or scooter to another, snapping their security chains with a big pair of bolt-cutters, while his van, its back doors thrown open, stands close at hand with its engine running.

The only way back into town is to retrace your steps. Walk straight ahead out of the market and you will return to Trastevere. Or turn right and walk across the **Ponte Sublicio** to come into Testaccio.

BATTELLI ROMANA: A TRIP ON THE TIBER

The Tiber is a surprise. Green as the leaves on the plane trees that line its banks, it is an almost empty river. It has the mood of a provincial waterway, quite out of character with the noisy, crowded city to either side. Lean over any of its central city bridges and watch water rats scurrying over the piers, small thickets of greenery where pigeons and gulls perch and fight, while the river eddies around arches and shallows. It is peaceful in a way that belies the Tiber's history as a difficult river.

Once, the Tiber was a place of ceremonial entrances, of triumphant displays of wealth and power. Emperors, popes and aristocrats came to their palaces and their city by boat and were watched by the masses. Armies strode over its bridges, breaking step to protect the structure, and battles were fought on and over them. The great and the grand built on the Tiber's banks and the trade of the city was conducted in ports and on slipways along its length. Great porticoes allowed impressive entrances by foreign dignitaries and protected merchants from the elements; and the people of Rome, when roused, threw their enemies, alive or dead, into the unforgiving waters. Bar a few ruins, all this is long gone.

In recent decades silting has been a problem and, as a

result, there has been virtually no river traffic. The increasing construction of bridges slowed the river's flow and contributed to the problems. But from antiquity to the late nineteenth century, flooding was also a fairly regular disaster. All over the city commemorative stones mark high-water levels at the times of great floods. Some are almost unimaginably high. The worst occurred in late spring as snow melted on the mountains beyond Rome but they could happen at any time since the Tiber draws its waters from far away. Currents were violent and treacherous. In October 1824 the sixteen-year-old Miss Rosa Bathurst fell from her horse into the Tiber and was instantly swept to her death. Six months later, her body was washed up and identified by her bonnet, rings and riding habit. She was buried in the Protestant Cemetery where her gravestone recounts the several misfortunes that befell her and her family **(Walk 6)**.

From time to time bridges were washed away. Some – for example, the **Ponte Sisto**, which spans the river from the Campo De' Fiori area to Trastevere – still have great circular tunnels cut through them to lessen the force of the rising river. Even today, when water reaches these apertures a flood warning is issued.

In the 1870s a programme began to build high embankments. This provided substantial alleviation of the almost annual flooding problem but at some cost. Many great houses had stretched down to the river or had had waterside gardens; the lovely Renaissance Villa Farnesina in Trastevere was one. Other areas had alleys and slipways, boatyards, quays and porticoes where water surged over the footings. All were obliterated by the improvements.

Since 2003 it has been possible to see the city from this historic river – not as previous generations did, but still permitting a rare view of some great monuments whose creators took this approach for granted. Boarding for boat trips is on the western side of **Tiber Island (Isola Tiberina)** on the Trastevere embankment at the **Calata degli Anguillara**, and the 75-minute journey up to the Duca d'Aosta Bridge is astonishingly good value at just one euro each way (stay on the boat to return). Boats leave just about hourly from 8.00 a.m. and the last trip back starts at 6.55 p.m. From **Ponte Marconi** it is equally possible to go downstream to Ostia.

The open-sided river boat chugs slowly upstream, playing music by Italy's answer to Edith Piaf. It gives a quite different perspective on Rome and on a hot day provides a perfect, cool vantage point to read or sunbathe. (Move swiftly to the front for this – the only uncovered seats are to either side of the captain's cabin.) There are no snacks and no drinks to be had on board so these need to be bought in advance, but there is a traditional kiosk on the embankment above the quay.

On the shore of the island people sunbathe on the stone and gulls dive for food. As the height of the embankment

Tiber bathing club

Anglers on the Tiber

hides much of ground-level Rome, from then on most of what one sees for a while is just the tops of trees, high river façades and grand rooflines. On a summer's day life down below, on the footpath along the bank, is simpler. Runners, mothers with children, trotting dogs and even three Buddhist monks walking in single file all enjoy the river breezes. Fishermen sit in clusters and the ubiquitous Roman lovers lie in tangles. Hopeful ducks bob in the wake of the boat or sleep on the river bank and the occasional fish leaps into the air.

Obvious on a map, the extent of the Tiber's meanderings is scarcely noticeable from the shore but viewed from the boat the bridges stretch ahead at different angles to each other, and the view forward is often blocked by the intrusion of a bulge of bank.

There is an official history told in bridges. Bridges commemorate murdered politicians or members of the royal House of Savoy, or radicals who were instrumental in bringing about the unification of Italy, but there are also bridges here built by the emperors and a couple built by Mussolini. The Ponte Fabricio, which dates from 62 BCE and joins the Isola Tiberina to the bank, is followed by the Ponte Garibaldi. Then comes the elegant sixteenth-century Ponte Sisto and the nineteenth-century Ponte G. Mazzini, Ponte Principe Savoia Aosta and Ponte Vittorio Emanuele II. Between the Principe Savoia Aosta and Vittorio Emanuele II bridges the foundation of a much older bridge, constructed by the Emperor Nero, can just be seen when the waters are low. Just before the Ponte Vittorio Emanuele II is one of the Tiber's finest riverscapes. Appearing through the plain broad span of the Vittorio Emanuele II bridge is the line of ornate angelic statues that line the parapet of the much older Ponte S. Angelo. Beside them, looming over the river, with the figure of the Archangel Michael in swirling draperies and brandishing a sword on its highest point, is the **Castel S. Angelo (Walk 9)**. There can be no finer spot from which to see it. It is possible to disembark here, explore the Castel and its museum and catch a later boat on up the river.

Turned into a fortress in the Middle Ages and later a prison – the imaginary location from which the operatic heroine Tosca leaps to her death – the hulk of the building can occasionally look like a rather battered power station. But it is in fact much older than it seems; it was originally built by the second-century emperor Hadrian as his mausoleum. If it dominates the modern city and the river, how much more of an impression must it have created when isolated in its original finery of bronze and marble?

Beyond the Ponte S. Angelo, between the 1895 Ponte Umberto and the 1901 Ponte Cavour, to the left, is the startling white tracery of the Gothic church of **Sacro Cuore del Suffragio (Walk 9)**. Not long after this the embankments start to diminish and very soon the river becomes a wide rural

Ponte Flaminio
Ponte Milvio
Ponte Duca d'Aosta
Ponte Risorgimento
Ponte Matteotti
Ponte Pietro Nenni
Ponte Regina Margherita
Ponte Cavour
Ponte Sant'Angelo
Ponte Umberto I
Ponte Vittorio Emanuele II
Ponte Principe
Amedeo di Savoia Aosta
Ponte Mazzini
Ponte Garibaldi
Ponte Fabricio
Ponte Sisto
Ponte Cestio
Ponte Rotto
Ponte Palatino
Ponte Sublicio
Ponte Testaccio
Ponte dell'
Industria
Ponte Marconi

River Tiber

waterway, running between fertile banks with bamboo thickets, bougainvillea, willow, plane and chestnut trees, and figs. Brambles run down to the edge and knotted roots descend through the water. A solitary cat tries to fish with its paw, ducklings scoot out from behind submerged logs, an otter splashes into the river. Soon come a scattering of boathouses, sturdy middle-aged men in all-too-brief thongs manhandling their canoes in and out of the water, some large houses set back behind shrubbery, and tennis courts. It could be a Mediterranean Twickenham. But in the distance purple hills rise steeply and cypresses dot the hillsides and at Ponte Duca d'Aosta the river-boat captain sounds his horn loudly after formally pulling into the little jetty: as with Adelstrop, no one leaves and no one comes or is ever likely to, so he lets his boat drift wide across the quiet river before it heads back towards the city centre.

*

St Peter's from the river

The views on the return trip from this surprisingly unfamiliar perspective are in many ways more impressive than those on the outward journey. The increasing grandeur of the sights as suburb turns to city, whether of stone Fascist eagles on a bridge, distant churches, the ridge of trees on the Janiculum Hill or, unforgettable if the return home is in the evening, the sun setting behind the great dome of **St Peter's** as the boat passes back under Ponte S. Angelo, can be breathtaking.

WALK 9
The Vatican

- Ponte S. Angelo
- Castel S. Angelo
- St Peter's
- Vatican City
- The Vatican Museums
- The Borgo and Prati districts
- S. Cuore dell' Suffragio
- The Museum of Dead Souls

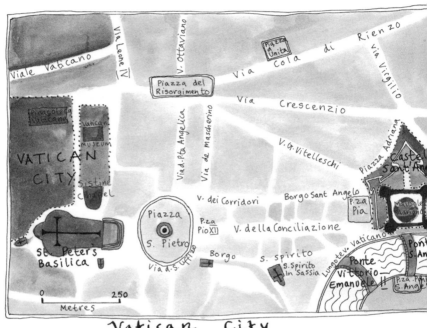

Vatican City

Rome is full of churches: they nudge each other on cramped streets, they nestle inside or over each other: new churches built in old churches, old churches built in pagan temples, temples built on shrines so ancient that they are beyond dating. Christianity has given Rome the grandiose façades with their proud inscriptions, the soft brick churches of early faith, the lovely cloisters hidden from traffic and commerce and the vast basilicas illuminated with incomparable artwork. And then there are the tiny, long-closed chantries sooty with neglect, the *madonnelli* on so many street corners: soft pink and blue Virgins, wreathed in flowers or clouds, borne up by cherubs. The street shrines with their red-glass candleholders and silver hearts, the street *names* – surely more than half the roads here are named after saints or their churches? The Egyptian obelisks, the triumphal columns of ancient emperors, the ebullience of pagan art, all confidently reclaimed in the name of Christ or his saints. But there are also elements that are much harder for an outsider to comprehend. The relics: the splinters of the True Cross, the bones of martyrs, the dried flesh of saints in glorious jewelled reliquaries, the beatifications, ecstasies, indulgences, scourges, the privations of monastic orders and the obsession with death, and often cruel death, that at times makes Catholicism, seen through its churches, seem like a death cult. But much of the geography, appearance and, although to a diminishing extent, culture of the modern city of Rome has been shaped by centuries of Catholicism.

After its heyday from the fifteenth to the eighteenth century, and after seeing off many previous threats, papal power finally retreated in the face of the nineteenth-century European movements of nationalism and anti-clericalism, forced back behind the walls of its base west of the Tiber. Today, the **Vatican City** is an independent state. Created in

1929, it is the smallest such in Europe – but it possesses the largest Christian basilica – **St Peter's** – in the world.

Behind its seventeenth-century ramparts, the Vatican has its own radio, newspapers, hospitals, bank, police, fire brigade, diplomats, mint, railway station, heliport and post office. It also has its own intrigues, gossip – and, inevitably, its own corruption.

It is the great Basilica of St Peter's that creates the spectacle that is at the centre of the Catholic Church. The dome of St Peter's is a landmark from almost every viewpoint in the city, from the Tiber, from the hills, through the keyhole of the Priory of the Knights of Malta, from ordinary apartment balconies and aeroplanes circling into Fiumcino and Ciampino airports. Approached across the Piazza San Pietro, it is a piece of breathtaking drama, whatever your personal beliefs. In earlier days pilgrims approached along the Via dei Coronari or,

St Peter's Basilica and appropriate road sign

later, the Via Giulia, especially laid out to permit their safe passage to St Peter's. Whatever your itinerary when you explore Rome, the best way to come into the Piazza S. Pietro is to walk across the **Ponte S. Angelo** as earlier pilgrims did. Or, only recently possible, to come by boat up the Tiber from Tiber Island, and get off at **Castel Sant' Angelo** (see **Walk 8**).

Animula vagula blandula
Hospes comesque corporis
Quae nunc abibis in loca
Pallidula, rigida, nudula,
Nec, et ut soles, dabis iocos.

O blithe little soul, thou, flitting away,
Guest and comrade of this my clay,
Whither now goest thou, to what place
Bare and ghastly and without grace?
Nor, as thy wont was, joke and play.

Hadrian's *Elegy to my departing soul*,
inscribed within his mausoleum: c. 130 CE

The bridge that leads straight to the looming fortress that is Castel Sant' Angelo – the great mausoleum of an emperor, later a papal stronghold – begins to set the scene. The ten statues of angels that line the bridge were designed by Bernini and added to the second-century structure fifteen hundred years after its original construction. Each one represents a different element in the Passion. These are strangely uneasy angels: there is something stormy in their curling and billowing draperies. But this has been a historically troubled spot. In ancient Rome the eastern side of the bridge was the approximate location of a place known as *Tarentum*, believed to be an entrance to the realm of the dead. Here sulphur emerged from a fissure in the earth and the gods of the underworld, Proserpina and Dis, were

Hadrian's Mausoleum

propitiated. In the sixteenth century it is where Beatrice Cenci, her brother and stepmother were executed. On one occasion in the fourteenth century hundreds of pilgrims were crushed to death on the bridge or drowned in the Tiber. On top of the Castel Sant' Angelo, the powerful bronze figure of the Archangel Michael brandishes his sword to protect the city.

Different nationalities seem to cluster around different attractions in Rome. There is probably an anthropological thesis in this. Americans have remained safely around the Spanish Steps since the nineteenth century, the French like the Forum and the more obscure churches, the British, Germans and Scandinavians queue for the Colosseum and dine – early – in Trastevere. The Japanese huddle round the Bocca di Verita. But the Italians too come to Rome as tourists, of course. They shop in the Via Condotti and survey Rome from the Janiculum, but Castel Sant' Angelo is their favourite tourist sight. It is understandable that this should be so. It contains the dust of a dead emperor, the sumptuous private rooms of popes, and sensual frescoes that speak of a very different climate of ecclesiastical power. The dankest of dungeons and displays of instruments of torture reflect its time as a state prison that served the popes and the repressive French regime of the early nineteenth century alike. Its trompe l'œil wall paintings have charm and wit. And, of course, there is that association with *Tosca*, one of the more passionate of grand operas. On the terrace there is both a fine view and an excellent, if pricey, café. It is a compressed history of Rome at its best, worst and most irresistible.

Turn left and walk down the **Via della Conciliazione**. The controversial construction of this thoroughfare, built between 1936 and 1950, swept away many of the narrow streets of the medieval Borgo. It has to some extent extended the sense of drama of the approach to St Peter's, although purists would vigorously disagree. Those who prefer the old effect of sudden wonderful shock rather than a long showy ceremonial can gain something of the spirit of the original experience by coming at the Piazza S. Pietro from the side, either approaching from the left of the Castel Sant' Angelo where the original corridor – the *passetto* – links the old papal apartments with St Peter's, coming in through the colonnades, or walking beside the river and up Borgo S. Spirito. This passes the still-working hospital of **S. Spirito** that dates from the thirteenth century and is the oldest in Rome. Here foundling infants could once be left in a rotating drum behind a grille. The drum still survives. What the approach up the Via della Conciliazione has lost in picturesqueness it has gained in a certain architectural didacticism, appropriate perhaps for an enterprise begun by Mussolini. Visitors are somehow funnelled in, drawn along and then delivered, awed, in front of St Peter's.

St Peter's Colonnade, dawn

As you come into Piazza S. Pietro another vast regiment of angels is lined up along the two piers of the colonnade. To come here at dawn is unforgettable as the sky lightens to reveal the vast dome of St Peter's and the emptiness of the piazza. The architecture is such that one's perspective is altered; even when full of crowds, it remains a daunting, humbling architectural space. In the centre is an ancient obelisk from Egypt that was erected here in 1586, and, to either side, slightly diminished by the proportions of everything around them, there are two seventeenth-century fountains, one by Maderno and one by Fontana.

In the far balcony are seen the two great showy peacock fans, and between them a figure clad in white, that rises from a golden chair and spreads his great sleeves like wings, as he raises his arms in benediction. That is the Pope, Pius the Ninth. All is dead silence, and a musical voice, sweet and penetrating, is heard chanting from the balcony; – the people bend and kneel; with a cold grey flash all the bayonets gleam as the soldiers drop to their knees, and rise to salute as the voice dies away, and the two white wings are again waved; – then thunder the cannon, – the bells clash and peal, – a few white papers, like huge snowflakes drop wavering from the balcony; – these are indulgences and there is an eager struggle for them below.

Story's *Roba di Roma* (C19)

Modern-day pilgrims still flock here but they are hordes brought by coach and dressed in easy-care clothes, not in the oilskin capes and carrying the pilgrim's staffs that helped them on the long walk across the *campagna* (the empty Roman countryside outside the city) in previous centuries. The coaches, brightly lettered and air-conditioned, and from every country in Europe, are parked nose to tail. And then there are the priests and the monks and the nuns dressed in every conceivable style and colour of habit from every corner of the globe and every type of society. Young African nuns in short white pleated dresses, chattering, smiling Filipina nuns in pale blue frocks, nuns swathed in the dignity of medieval black and wearing crisp wimples, nuns in pale brown cotton, their grey hair waved back off their faces. Older Italian women greet nuns of their

Papal crown fountain, Vatican

own age with a respectful 'Buongiorno, Madre'. Friars and monks: Franciscans in brown (or the Franciscans of Assisi who have reverted to dark grey – in linen with a mobile-phone pocket), Benedictines in black and Cistercians in white.

But it is not just the officially devout who flock here: more than at any other site in Rome there are tourists here of every age and nationality. They come and they queue. They queue with babies in arms in the full sun, they queue in the wind and the rain, they queue for as long as they are required to queue. The religious and aesthetic treasures on display are of such quality and number that better arrangements have never needed to be made. The Swiss Guard stand, handsome and halberded in their Renaissance uniforms whose reds, yellows and bright blues are startling against the white and grey of the buildings that their wearers protect. But the *Carabinieri* patrol the square

Swiss guards

too, guns in holsters, and the *Vigilanza* is the Vatican's own police force. The strange presence of a personal bodyguard selected from young male Catholic nationals from a strongly Protestant nation is historic. The Swiss Guard originally earned their position through their courage and loyalty in protecting Pope Clement VII against The Holy Roman Emperor in 1527. Recruited from the Cantons of Switzerland, many stay here when their tour of duty is done. One ex-Guardsman is a florist, running one of Rome's most glamorous flower shops. For all the visible tradition, the attempted assassination of the pope in 1981, the still slightly opaque double murder and suicide involving members of the Swiss Guard in 1998, and the sheet of bulletproof glass in front of Michelangelo's exquisitely moving *Pietà* in St Peter's are all reminders that the Vatican is as vulnerable to acts of violence as any other modern state.

●

I went out, and almost ran to St Peter's. I would not look to the right or left, (I know I passed through Piazza Navona,) till I came to the Colonnades and there was the first ray of the rising sun just touching the top of the fountain. The Civic guard was just exercising in the Piazza. The dome was much smaller than I expected. But that enormous Atrio. I stopped under it, for my mind was out of breath, to recover strength before I went in. No event in my life, except my death can ever be greater than that first entrance into St Peter's, the concentrated spirit of Christianity which is the worship of grief. I went in.

Florence Nightingale *Letters from Rome* (1848)

●

Inside it is the dome, Michelangelo's masterpiece, that astonishes first, taking the eye upwards and diverting the mind from the wonder of God to the wonder of Man and the extraordinary achievement of design, engineering and artistry that raised it. The basilica is vast but its effects are not created primarily by size – it would be unimaginable for it to be left uncluttered, like the Pantheon. Instead, it is an immense cave of treasure: that mixture of glittering gold and rich colour in an enclosed darkness that is so much a feature of great Catholic churches. All this despite its 233 windows. Those who discuss St Peter's invariably do so in terms of its size; in all its constituent parts it is simply bigger than anything else and so, with little to compare it to, the dizzying numbers become almost meaningless. The tip of the cross mounted on the cupola is 448 feet above ground, the nave is 613 feet long, even the portico is a massive 468 feet from end to end. Six hundred workmen constructed the dome. There are 46 altars.

The interior of St Peter's is too well endowed with religious art and artefacts to be covered here in detail and information on site is comprehensive. But although individual items are of staggering beauty and artistry – the *Pietà*, the baldacchino, the Confessional Altar at which only the pope may celebrate Mass, even the Stuart memorials – it is with the sum of its parts that it makes its impact. Nothing ever surpasses the moment of first entry.

There are odd and charming eccentricities: the mummified body of the early-twentieth-century Pope Pius X lying in a crystal case like Snow White, the series of depictions of a woman's face as she experiences maternity from conceiving a child to giving birth, sculpted by Borromini and surrounding the baldacchino, the sweet excess of the rococo tomb of Marie Clementina Sobieski, James Stuart's – the Pretender's – wife. What is in some ways stranger than the pomp and beauty that surrounds worshippers at ground level is that the basilica sits not just on the ruins of the earlier church, built by Constantine, but on a necropolis. What is under the church is almost as fascinating as what is inside it: crypts, grottoes, whole naves, floors and fragments of the original church and,

Statuary, St Peter's

of course, tombs, including the supposed burial place of St Peter himself. And they are still digging. What is on high competes, too: an enormous vista over Rome can be seen by those with a head for heights and the stamina to climb beyond the internal gallery of the dome to the lantern.

Whatever else they may be the collected buildings of the Vatican form one of the greatest museums on earth. The entrance to the miles of galleries that make up the Vatican museums, including the **Sistine Chapel** and the **Raphael Rooms**, is off Viale Vaticano. This is at some distance from St Peter's and leads off the Via S. Pellegrino, to the right as you face St Peter's. Seeing the Sistine Chapel comes at a price. You may queue to enter, be crushed when you get inside, be silenced by stern priests and processed through at some speed. At the centre of the experience is the controversial restoration. There is, still, a wonder in Michelangelo's virtuosity and a shock at seeing many familiar images previously viewed only in reproduction, and this somehow transcends – just – the rather impersonal experience of viewing them. Anyway, not to see the bright colours and definition that emerged from the restoration in context is not to have a valid opinion. The secret, although it is a secret known to more than a few, to enjoying the ceiling and frescoes of the chapel with a degree of serenity is to arrive well before the doors to the Vatican Museums open. Enter as they open and walk through the collections without being seduced to linger in front of the other temptations on show. They are many, but you can return to them. Go straight to the chapel.

St Catherine in a green gown, and somebody else in a blue one are supremely hideous. Paul IV, in an unfortunate fit of prudery, was seized with the resolution of whitewashing over the whole of *The Last Judgement* in order to cover the scandal of a few naked female figures. With difficulty was he prevented from utterly destroying the grandest painting in the world, but he could not be dissuaded from ordering that these poor women be clothed in this unbecoming drapery.

Eaton's Rome (C19)

Michael Angelo avenged himself on Messer Biagio da Cesena, master of the ceremonies, who first suggested the indelicacy of naked figures to the Pope, by introducing him in hell, as Midas, with ass's ears.

Augustus Hare *Walks in Rome*

No one could ever encompass all that the **Vatican Museums** contain in a single book, much less a chapter, nor see it all in a day or even a week. Although its treasures are many, it is easy to become dispirited by the sheer size of the museums and the volume of acquisition. With limited time to spare concentrate on the **Raphael Rooms**, the octagonal courtyard of the **Museo Pio Clementino** – which is charming in itself and which, with its surrounding rooms, holds the most famous of the classical collections (the zoo of animal statuary is particularly fun) – and the **Belvedere Museum**, the first purpose-built/designed gallery for sculpture. The gallery of the **Pinacoteca** is a possibility if you still have the energy for a relentless array of religious art. The museum of modern religious art is less compelling. It is a work of architecture that makes the greatest modern contribution here: the graceful helical ramp by Giuseppe Momo that leads from the museums to the street below. Looking down from the top is like looking into the perfect whorl of a shell.

> The three rooms occupied by the pontiff are furnished with a simplicity which would be inconceivable in the abode of any other sovereign prince. The furniture is confined to the merest necessaries of life; strange contrast to Lambeth and Fulham!
>
> Augustus Hare *Walks in Rome*

The Vatican is well protected and the gardens can only be seen from an organized bus tour. Unless you have a yearning for the aerial delights of the Pope's bees (in the flesh, not – for once – in stone) or the Pope's heliport, there are many other lovely gardens in Rome that are more easily and intimately enjoyed than these.

Reeling from the display of religiously inspired aesthetic wonders, anyone leaving the Vatican is assailed by the souvenir stands. There has always been a market in souvenirs and travellers have always complained about the price. The **Via dei Coronari**, once the major approach road to St Peter's,

Bargain religious memorabilia

is named after the rosary sellers who once plied their trade along it. Rosaries are still a staple of the local gift shops. The more modern souvenirs bring Catholic iconography out of the museums and into modern culture but, in so doing, entangle it with the pagan past as well as bursting exuberantly through the bounds of good taste. There are T-shirts with Christ crucified, where an optical illusion lets his eyes open and close, his head fall to the side. The Pope extends his blessing from within a plastic snowstorm or, with a supernatural degree of poise, from the top of Michelangelo's dome. Lollipop popes, plaster-of-Paris popes, resin basilicas that look like small iced cakes.

The Vatican itself has, finally, caught up with the merchandising opportunities discovered by the other great museums of the world and does now have its own shop at Via delle Grazie 13, selling items that are elegant, reverent and well made; but they are scarcely the stuff, or the price, of the spontaneous purchase. Still, they would make fine god-parental presents for a baptism.

The Vatican does not exist in isolation on the west bank of the river. However, it is true that its ambience is remarkably contained and that once outside its walls its immediate influence and the sense of its presence disappear swiftly. It is, appropriately enough, a place to be seen from afar, or from above, from an aeroplane.

The remnants of the medieval **Borgo**, through which Mussolini cut his uncompromising swathe with the Via della Conciliazione, still survive between the Vatican and Castel Sant' Angelo. These streets and small squares with their fountains still have charm and are a good place to walk around in and to sit and recover from a morning in the Vatican Museums. The word 'Borgo' is taken from the German *burg* and this was once an area of taverns and inns that accommodated pilgrims. Today the few local pizzerias and *osteria* serve unpretentious everyday Roman food but *Taverna Angelica* at Piazza A. Capponi 6 is a notable, if more expensive, exception, specializing in fish and other food prepared with a light and imaginative touch. The rooms have an understated style, music is low and a sophisticated kitchen produces some really exceptional and unusual dishes, modern takes on the oldest of ingredients: tagliolini with squid; prawns with valerian, pineapple and ginger; a plate of duck prepared in three ways (smoked, roasted and tartare); breast of goose with orange; turbot with capers; and some cool, creamy and delicious puddings – dates with coffee cream, for instance. The cheeses are excellent but the classic apple tart with ice cream is of a flavour and delicacy that justifies coming to the area simply to eat.

The same could be said for *Velando*, at Borgo Vittorio 26, which specializes in food from Val Comonica in northern

Italy. It too combines the best of *nouvelle cuisine* with the more robust flavours of classic Italian cooking and seasonal ingredients, including some unusual varieties of home-made pasta. There is plenty for the vegetarian here, too: aubergine with fresh tomatoes, bean purée and chicory as a starter, for instance, and puddings such as citrus fruit *bavarois* and strawberry risotto are the house specialities. There is a sense of friendly professionalism and calm here that makes the sight of the odd discreet prelate seem not at all surprising.

Another night-time return visit should be to *Alexanderplatz* at Via Ostia 9, close to the entrance to the Vatican Museums. This is simply the best jazz and blues club in Rome, at its most atmospheric on a winter's night. But it is fun at any time and in summer it moves outside to the magical surroundings of the Villa Celimontana on the Celian Hill **(Walk 7)**. Two quite different locations and the same wonderfully innovative music by top names.

The **Prati** district lies beyond this and has a further selection of slightly smarter restaurants. *Il Matriciano* at Via dei Gracchi 55 is traditional but accomplished and is garnished unabashedly with photographs of wartime derring-do in the Axis forces. It serves tiny rice dumplings in broth and some of the best *pasta all'amatriciana* anywhere. Prati was developed after the reunification of Italy in 1870 and is a stolid area of apartment blocks, regularly laid out. It has become an affluent suburb, slightly muffled in its feel. In winter ladies who lunch do so in their furs and there is a degree of refinement about the occasional *pasticceria* here which is more akin to Italy's northern cities – appropriately, perhaps, as the area was originally strongly Piedmontese in allegiance and style. But there are some good hotels in this area and some superior bed-and-breakfast accommodation.

*

To leave the Vatican, it is best to return by the Ponte Sant' Angelo. But, if you have time, a quick walk away along the embankment in the opposite direction from St Peter's, along the Lungotevere Prati, is one of the more strange manifestations of faith. The church of **S. Cuore del Suffragio** is a rare example of Gothic architecture in Rome. It stands, almost crystalline in its whiteness and its spires, on the bank of the Tiber.

Next to it is the **Museum of the Souls of the Dead**. The bizarre exhibits are the visible signs, usually conveyed by fire, sent by the dead in Purgatory to exhort the living to pray for their souls. They include a nightcap with a man's dead wife's handprint burned onto it as well as furniture, clothing, Bibles and linen all clearly scorched. Fingerprints darken the pages of a prayer book, a nun's tunic has the burned residue of clutching fingers. On the wall the face of a soul in Purgatory looks down. The museum may yet be shut down as the nature of religious belief has changed dramatically since the collection was first displayed in the late nineteenth century: those who visit are often more morbidly curious than devout.

Turn back to the Ponte S. Angelo or cross the Tiber by the next bridge, Ponte Cavour, and reach another imperial mausoleum, this time of the first and greatest emperor of all, Augustus **(Walk 3)**.

S. Cuore del Suffragio (from the Tiber)

Appian Way

WALK 10

The Appian Way

- Baths of Caracalla
- Church of S. Giovanni a Porta Latina and Oratory of S. Giovanni in Oleo
- The Columbarium of Pomponius Hylas and the Tomb of the Scipios
- The Catacombs
- The Fosse Ardeatine Memorial
- The Caffarella and Nymphaeum of Egeria
- The Circus of Maxentius
- Tomb of Romulus
- Tomb of Cecilia Metella
- Tombs of the Via Appia Antica

Ruined façade, Via Appia

It is strange that one of the aspects of Rome that is most evocative of the past is a walk along a single road that leads with surprising swiftness from the hectic pace of a modern built-up city, through one of its ancient gates, to quiet countryside. It is a long walk, and most visitors will have to choose just one section to follow, but, particularly in its further reaches, it is an excellent counterpoint to days spent exploring central Rome. The air is fresh, the traffic is minimal, and sites of interest are well spread out. Once out of the city, the surroundings are recognizably the same ruins and villas set in fields that many travellers of previous centuries have found peaceful and beautiful, if touched with melancholy. This is the **Via Appia**, or **Appian Way**, first laid down in 312 BCE. Along its length there are ruined tombs, deserted churches and famous catacombs.

In antiquity the Via Appia was considered a desirable location to live. The philosopher and writer Seneca, the wealthy Herodes Atticus, the playwright Terence and many others had estates nearby. Modern life still continues in the scattered houses of those lucky – and rich – enough to live here. Some fine old villas standing behind high walls or glimpsed momentarily at the end of long drives or in abundant gardens have ancient ruins in their grounds and one or two roadside farmhouses have ancient tombs incorporated into their structures. There is also a nineteenth-century fort, still an active military base, by the side of the road where legionaries once marched. A handful of restaurants serve hearty lunches and dinners to Roman families, and the few churches here are fashionable locations for weddings; on summer evenings processions of cars, with guests in evening dress, clutching beautifully wrapped presents, can be seen bumping very slowly down the uneven stones and ruts of the old road.

This was once known as the Queen of Roads. Its best-preserved sections reveal its relatively narrow width – four metres – just enough for five soldiers marching abreast, or one cart passing in each direction. At the height of Rome's growth, one wagon of building materials rumbled into the city from the Via Appia every minute. Triumphant Roman armies marched along it, and it was a crucial conduit for trade. From Republican times onwards monumental tombs and catacombs were built to either side.

Rome was, by the standards of its time, a vast city, and the

Roman wheel ruts on the Via Appia

problem of disposing of its dead was acute, exacerbated by the regulation that human remains should be buried outside the city. Most burials were beside major roads. Famous or very wealthy citizens might start building an individual or family monument before their death and while affluent families had great family tombs or decorated sepulchres, the ashes of slaves or the poor might be stacked one on top of another, in a shape that became known as a *columbarium* (dovecote).

So common are surviving *columbaria* that they occasionally get pressed into uses that their original owners could never have dreamed of. One is incorporated into a drugstore in Trastevere, others into houses on the Via Appia. Perhaps one of the most unusual locations is at Via Appia 87 where a large columbarium contains one of the oldest restaurants in Rome. It has long intrigued visitors; Piranesi and Goethe both came here.

Beautifully restored, though with its roof long gone, with its tumbling creepers and the faint smell of jasmine it might feel like a very old high-walled garden were it not for the imposing ranks of niches. *Hosteria Antica* has rather a self-conscious sense of the past: this is a restaurant with its own history book and press cuttings, and guests are handed postcards portraying the owners as cartoon ancient Romans, lounging on their couch. But the place has great charm, notwithstanding. It is peaceful and rather elegant: by day a canvas awning protects the tables from the sun, by night there is unobtrusive guitar music. The owners are friendly and helpful in their enthusiasm and the menu is broad – excellent fish, interesting vegetables – and contains one main course (chicken-based) and one pudding (eggs, nuts, honey and black pepper) straight from the alleged first-century cookbook of Apicius. Both are surprisingly good. The wine list is more conventional, though comprehensive.

Up to the fifth century many Romans were buried in **catacombs**. These have been found all around the city. Sometimes the galleries of old quarries were used for this purpose and at others new chambers were dug: previously uncharted ones still emerge when major building schemes dig deep near old routes out of the city. This form of interment was used for early Romans and for the Jewish community but it became especially popular with early Christians who were ideologically averse to cremation. For a long time it was believed that they also held services in the catacombs to avoid persecution but in fact this was not so: traces of eating and the smoke from ancient lamps are simply the residues of families returning to visit and honour their dead. The trade of catacomb-digger was an honoured one and, between them, the cumulative length of the galleries of those catacombs that have been discovered runs to hundreds of kilometres. The tombs and the saintly relics connected with them became a destination for pilgrims until the Middle Ages.

By medieval times the strategic as well as the symbolic importance of the Via Appia caused the Caetani family to acquire the most famous monument – the huge tomb of **Cecilia Metella** – and turn it into a fortress to control the road and extract taxes from those who used it. This act of appropriation was one factor in the surprising survival of much of the Via Appia in its original condition. Pragmatic Romans simply established an alternative route and eventually a new road, the **Appia Nuova**, took the brunt of the traffic. The old Appian Way became a wild, neglected and forgotten place. It was only in the early nineteenth century that Antonio Canova began to champion the beauty of the ancient funerary monuments. A little later the catacombs were rediscovered and a whole new tourist attraction opened up.

There is a stern round tower of other days
Firm as a fortress, with its fence of stone,
Such as an army's baffled strength delays
Standing with half its battlements alone,
And with two thousand years of ivy grown,
The garland of eternity, where wave
The green leaves over all by time o'erthrown; –
What was this tower of strength? Within its cave
What treasure lay so lock'd, so hid – a woman's grave.

Byron, *Childe Harold*

Today not all catacombs are open to the public, though special permits can be obtained for some of the others – with some difficulty and plenty of advance warning – from the Pontifical Commission for Sacred Archaeology at Via Napoleon III, number 1.

The most popular catacombs are this cluster on the Appian Way, including the **Catacombs of S. Callisto**, **S. Sebastiano** and **Domitilla**. These can all be crowded in high season and the upper levels have suffered a bit from their years as tourist attractions. Via Nomentana and Salaria in the north-west also have good catacombs and fewer visitors **(Walk 5)**.

The road is very different in mood at different parts along its length and the section from central Rome to the ring road is several miles long so that only the sturdiest walker is likely to cover it all. From the **Baths of Caracalla** running up to the **Porta S. Sebastiano** the road itself (it is called the Via di Porta S. Sebastiano at this point) is picturesque, passing between high stone walls overhung by trees, but the experience is rather spoiled by the last stretch which has no pavement at all. Here traffic hurtles by at breathtaking speed and the width of the road makes pedestrian options very limited. However, on Sundays all motor traffic is banned and the whole road is transformed.

The **Baths of Caracalla** merit a visit all on their own. The substantial remains evoke the immensity of the original complex of baths, gymnasium, library and sculpture galleries that served Ancient Rome from the third century CE until the Goths cut the aqueducts in the sixth. The Baths accommodated up to 10,000 people in their echoing halls. They were rich in works of art, many of which are now scattered throughout Rome and not just in museums; the great granite fountains of the cold rooms now ornament the Piazza Farnese **(Walk 1)**. There were beautifully observed mosaic illustrations of boxers, athletes, gladiators and their trainers; there were coloured marbles and glass mosaics, and bronze sheeting lined the ceiling. Originally the outside too was decorated with coloured glass. The effect from a distance must have been quite extraordinary. It would have been seen, smelled and heard all over the surrounding area, a noisy, humid, brash manifestation of the culture and confidence of Ancient Rome.

By the early nineteenth century, it had quite another role. In its state of organic decay – half rocky outcrop covered in vegetation, half monument to the fall of great empires – it delighted the contemplative Romantic.

●

This poem was chiefly written upon the mountainous ruins of the Baths of Caracalla, among the flowery glades and thickets of odiferous trees, which are extended in ever-winding labyrinths upon its immense platforms and dizzy arches suspended in the air.

Percy Bysshe Shelley *Introduction to Prometheus Unbound* (1819)

●

Today, stripped of its vegetation, it has lost both the exuberance of antiquity and its disintegrating 'poetic' charm. It is, however, an awesomely large ruin: seagulls still treat it like a massive cliff and it is seen at its best when it hosts summer opera in the evenings.

Moving on from the Baths across the broad intersection that is the Piazzale Numa Pompilio, two roads lead from a bifurcation right to the walls of Rome. This walk continues down the one to the left-hand side. This is the quiet **Via Porta di Latina**, which climbs gently up a quiet residential street, hemmed in between old flint and brick walls, gardens and parkland. The only sound is birdsong.

There is one very pretty church up here: the eleventh-century **S. Giovanni a Porta Latina**, small and graceful in old brick with lights filtered milkily through selenite window-panes. A ninth-century well-head stands under a cedar outside and there are medieval fragments hung in the porch. A little beyond this is the **Oratorio S. Giovanni in Oleo**, erected in 1509 and restored by Borromini 150 years later. Here St John made his apparently miraculous escape from being boiled in oil. It is a tiny octagonal chapel, rarely open, that stands right by the robust old Porta Latina in the Aurelian Wall.

A small park lies through a gate immediately to the right, still within the walls. It is a rather forlorn, shady place of perpetual autumn, with fallen leaves thick on the grass, but within it the **Tomb of Pomponius Hylas** has wall-paintings, stucco and glass mosaics that are still bright. Ask the caretaker to take you in. Walking across the park downhill, you come out by way of steps and another gate, turning right straight onto the Via di Porta S. Sebastiano, which becomes the Via Appia immediately after the city gate. Immediately to the left, though, is an impressive sepulchre, the **Tomb of the Scipios**, the famous Roman family, one of whom defeated Hannibal.

After five minutes' walk, two arches cross the road. The first one you reach, coming from the city centre, is called the **Arch of Drusus** and was not a city gate but was built in the third century to carry an aqueduct. The **Porta S. Sebastiano** itself is in good repair and has some centuries-old graffiti, mostly religious in content, carved on it. Within the gate there is a small museum of the city walls and this is one of the few places where it is possible to walk right along them, in a westerly direction; the view is splendid. In the Second World War a senior member of the Fascist party liked it so much

Milestone, Via Appia Antica

that he made his office here. The gate which Roman legions returned through was also chosen, with a fine sense of the dramatic, as the route of entry for the liberating Allied forces in June 1944.

From this point onwards the area is now designated a national park, although it has lost none of its out-of-the-way charm because of this. Although the beginning of the second section from the Porta S. Sebastiano as far as the **Circus of Maxentius** is unattractively built up, there are ancient remains even here, between the lock-ups and the workshops, including an original milestone just beyond the wall and also an office for the whole **Park of the Appia Antica**, open on Sundays at Via Appia 42, with exhibitions, advice, details of guided tours and even bike hire for adults or children.

This stretch from the old gates includes the church of **Quo**

Vadis Domine and the much-visited catacombs of **S. Callistus** and **S. Sebastian**. Catacombs are not for the claustrophobic but nor are they at all sinister. Evenly cool, slightly damp and at times quite cramped as the passages narrow in places, all require a guide who will escort visitors through what are sometimes many levels of seemingly identical rock corridors, their walls pierced by thousands of niches – the *loculi* – in which bodies were once deposited. Many of these guides are extremely knowledgeable English-speakers and tailor their talks both to their own religious beliefs and to the party they are accompanying. Seeing just one catacomb provides a good sense of the whole, but it is in the detail that a faint echo of the people who once used them, who grieved at the loss of those they loved or celebrated their lives, survives.

In some ways it is the side roads that lead to the most atmospheric if lesser-known sites. To the right the Via Ardeatine leads to the **Catacombs of Domitilla** and the sombre memorial and museum of the **Fosse Ardeatine**, a quarry where, in March 1944, the occupying Nazi forces shot 335 civilians in reprisal for a bomb detonated by Italian partisans, which killed thirty-three German troops in Via Rasello. The tunnel was blown up, leaving the victims' bodies inside. It has since been cleared and the entrance has fine gates and modern sculptures by Coccia and Basaldella. Today each body lies in an individual tomb with its age, name and photograph mounted on top. It seems an appropriate resting place so near to the catacombs of so many much earlier Romans.

●

At first sight like a Christmas tree half lit up. These tiny lights – one on every coffin – and all these flowers, whole tunnel a vista of colour. Crossroads now and the same thing again – another vista of flowers and how fresh they look; like an underground conservatory. Or a bit like a maze of mirrors you find in a fun-fair. Tunnels crossing each other – and each reflecting the other.

Louis MacNeice 'On the Ardeatine Caves'
Portrait of Rome (1947)

To the right are the occasional relics of a vast estate that once spread along the Appian Way. The second-century CE Greek, **Herodes Atticus**, was an enormously rich man. In Athens and in Rome he used his fortune to build and the villas and gardens here were everything one could expect in an age of conspicuous consumption. However, the death in childbirth of his wife, the patrician Roman heiress Annia Regilla, provoked an outpouring of grief and funerary display. Some believe that the whole estate was turned into a monument to his dead spouse, dedicated to the gods of the underworld, with the extensive coloured decoration of his villa being replaced by black marble. Annia Regilla's alleged tomb is the ruined building known as the **Temple of Divus Rediculus** that sits in the gentle and forgotten valley of the little **River Almone**. This area is known as the **Caffarella** and is a sliver of ancient landscape between the Via Appia and the Via Latina, ending in a strange disjunction between the rural past and the edge of the modern city. Much of it once belonged to the Torlonia family but appropriation, legal intervention and efforts from pressure groups saved it from development. Fortified farmhouses, fragments of ruin, the medieval towers of eleventh-century fulling mills, a *columbarium* also used as a mill at one time, and, still, the occasional flock of rather shaggy sheep and goats are all caught in this place out of time. From the valley sides the hills around Rome can be seen and on a clear day in winter peaks dusted with snow are visible.

To find the Caffarella, follow the **Appia Pignatelli**, a road that forks off the Via Appia, and shortly afterwards take the rough lane, also to the left, along which is signposted the church of **St Urban**. This little church has an interesting interior, its classical past as a pagan temple to Ceres and Faustina wrapped in Christian trappings, including some particularly good frescoes. At present, however, there is no public access.

Just beyond here is one of the delights of this area. This is the ruin of the **Nymphaeum of Egeria**, little visited now but very popular with Romantic travellers. Newly restored, the nymphaeum has crumbled a little but not changed greatly from how it appeared in the prints of the eighteenth century. A pool and a vaulted grotto, surrounded by lush greenery and the remains of a statue, still have a certain magic in the sound of running water and cicadas. Greater Rome is not far away yet here Ancient Rome feels closer. The grotto has been dated to the second century CE and was probably a garden room of Herodes Atticus, possibly for dining in the heat of a summer's evening.

Nymphaeum of Egeria, Cafferella

Modern analysis has evoked the cool, humid beauty of its original state. The walls were green marble, the floor was of darkest green porphyry, the niches were lined in white marble, probably filled with statues and running water, and there were slim bands of decorative mosaic. In places, porous pumice stone encouraged moss and ferns to become established.

The **Temple of Divus Rediculus** (access on Sundays only), in reality probably not Annia Regilla's resting place but another *columbarium*, is a little beyond this, as is a tiny bridge over the river which marks what was once a major crossing on the road joining the two ancient highways of the Via Appia and the Via Latina. To return to the Appian Way either go back past the church of St Urban or take any turning further on to exit right from the Caffarella.

●

Dorothea had now been five weeks in Rome, and in the kindly mornings when autumn and winter seemed to go hand in hand like a happy aged couple one of whom would presently survive in chiller loneliness, she had driven about at first with Mr Casaubon, but of late chiefly with Tantripp and their experienced courier. She had been led through the best galleries, had been taken to the chief points of view, had been shown the grandest ruins and the most glorious churches, and she had ended by oftenest choosing to drive out to the Campagna where she could feel alone with the earth and sky, away from the oppressive masquerade of ages, in which her own life too seemed to become a masque with enigmatical costumes.

George Eliot *Middlemarch* (1871)

●

The next major monument on the Via Appia Antica is the **Villa and Circus of Maxentius**. From there to the sixth milestone at the junction with Via di Casal Rotondo the Via Appia is at its loveliest and most timeless, and is known as the Appia Antica (to distinguish it from the Appia Nuova). The bulk of the traffic on roads to the left and right disappears and there is a sudden peace (considerably more peace than the area would have known in antiquity). There are hawks over the fields, a rookery in a cluster of trees, and wild flowers: cobalt-blue geraniums, poppies and buttercups still blooming into high summer, while umbrella pines and cypresses frame the rutted basalt stones that stretch away to purple-grey mountains.

For those with limited resources of time or energy this is the most rewarding section of the Via Appia to walk. The easiest way do this, although you will miss out the city walls, catacombs and Caffarella, is to take a taxi to the tomb of Cecilia Metella. The driver will normally stop in the large lay-by beside the restaurant of the same name, a short distance from the monument itself. Alternatively, the number 118 bus will drop you a few metres further along. Ask for the *Villa di Massenzio*. Buses run from Pyramide or the Piazza Porta S. Giovanni. The *Restaurant Cecilia Metella* sits in rose gardens just before Maxentius's Villa. The approach through its car park and the sprawling terrace under its canopy give a slightly misleading first impression of this highly traditional restaurant, provincial in feel and menu and dominated by the looming first-century BCE mausoleum of Cecilia Metella herself. It is not so much tourists who come here but Roman families. Sometimes it is quiet in the shade of the vines, with cats prowling under the bushes and crickets in the olive trees: a good place for a slow lunch with good house wine. At other times there may be long and busy tables, music, dancing and numerous children celebrating a wedding party late into the night. The waiters are old hands and keen to suggest extra dishes based on what is fresh into the kitchens but the predictably named pasta Cecilia Metella with cream, ham and tiny peas is particularly good.

The spread of early fourth-century buildings around **Maxentius's Villa** is extensive. Today their remains stand in cornfields, sometimes with haystacks between the ruins. The circus is far better preserved, though smaller, than the more familiar Circus of Maximus. Here the towers which once supported the starting gates and the *spina* – the barrier that ran down the middle of the track – and the judges' box all survive. **The tomb of Maxentius's heir**, **Romulus**, aged four at

Tomb of Cecilia Metella

the time of his death, lies just to the west, partly concealed by a farmhouse. The whole complex might have been built on the estate that had once been the property of Herodes Atticus.

Cecilia Metella's tomb was always a monument to wealth and power although its twelfth-century reuse by the Caetani family as an expression of *their* wealth and power extended and changed the look of the structure: they added the fortifications to the side and the crenellations around the roof. Nevertheless, the sculptured frieze of bulls' skulls and garlands that still circles the tower is original (and gave the immediate area its name: *Capo di Bove*) as is the impressive bulk of this mausoleum of one woman. It can be visited and contains fragments of tombs found all along the Appian Way and there is another excellent view from the top, but it often shuts earlier than the official time of closing.

From the tower onwards, the road becomes increasingly rural. Fields stretch away to woods on the right and the Alban and Sabine mountains appear, hazily, in the distance. To the left, far away across the fields, modern Rome rises up abruptly in tower blocks and chimneys, as mysterious and unreal as the mountains. The single local shop at Via Appia 210, just by the second turning to Via Appia Pignatelli, is small, friendly and packed with good, ordinary food: a wide range of traditional breads, which the owner will often let you taste, cured meats, cheese, sweet-smelling lumpy tomatoes and bottled drinks. Assemble lunch here from fresh ingredients. The traditional *rosetta*, the ubiquitous breakfast roll which rather puzzles non-Italians, being all crust around a virtually empty interior, could not be better for a picnic, stuffed with cheese and ham and carried in the hand.

Long scavenged for their marble, most of the monumental tombs that once lined the road are either gone or reduced to single crumbling towers or numerous brick tumuli covered with vegetation. But there are exceptions. Every so often an unpromising mound turns out to be a small *columbarium*, often with the entrance hidden at the back, where underground niches

Walking towards the Campagna, Via Appia

once held the ashes of long-dead citizens of Rome. A handful of tombs have surviving reliefs, statuary or inscriptions, and others have been restored. The **Tomb of Festoons** has decoration that in places looks as clear as it was on the day when the mason carved it nearly two thousand years ago: the inscription lamenting the death of a mother and her two young children is still poignant. A rather less well-preserved statue of a young man, naked but for a cloak and, on a summer's evening, a wasp's nest in his armpit, is known as the **Heroic Relief**. The pleasing, but not original, pastiche of fragments on the left was assembled by the sculptor Canova. The **Tomb of Seneca**, although it probably never contained the man himself, is nevertheless a satisfyingly picturesque ivy-draped tower. Another tomb has allusions to Egyptian priestly connections, another stern-looking portrait of the family of Ilarius Fuscus. For those with stamina or a car, beside the fifth milestone stands the memorial to the seventh-century BCE Horatii brothers, two of whom died fighting at this spot. Then, looming across pastureland, rise the still-magnificent skeleton structures of the **Villa of the Quintilli**, two other unfortunate brothers who were executed by the Emperor Commodus in the second century.

Most walkers will probably have chosen to turn back long before this point. Although there are a few ruins, including the circular **Casal Rotondo** and an old inn and baths, at the sixth milestone, there is little else worth seeing, and less than a mile beyond this is a road to the left which eventually connects with the Via Appia Nuova. The Via Appia does continue as far as the ring road but the prostitutes and their car-driving clients who linger at this end make it less safe and less peaceful.

Perhaps the best way to see even a little bit of the Appian Way is to walk out in late afternoon from the Circus of Maxentius and to return as the sun is setting. It is extraordinarily evocative. The pine trees turn from dark green to black, the sky flames over the fields and trees, the castellations of the Tomb of Cecilia Metella are jagged against the sky. As the road falls towards Rome owls hoot from behind the roofless Gothic church of S. Nicola in Bari and oil lamps on the ground light the entrances to houses as they always have.

●

We wandered out upon the Appian Way, and then went on, through miles of ruined tombs and broken walls, with here and there a desolate and uninhabited house: past the Circus of Romulus, where the course of the chariots, the stations of the judges, competitors, and spectators, are yet as plainly to be seen as in old time: past the tomb of Cecilia Metella: past all inclosure, hedge, or stake, wall or fence: away upon the open Campagna, where on that side of Rome, nothing is to be beheld but Ruin. Except where the distant Apennines bound the view upon the left, the whole wide prospect is one field of ruin. Broken aqueducts, left in the most picturesque and beautiful clusters of arches; broken temples; broken tombs. A desert of decay, sombre and desolate beyond all expression; and with a history in every stone that strews the ground.

Charles Dickens *Pictures of Italy*

●

OPENING TIMES FOR MUSEUMS, MONUMENTS AND GALLERIES

All museums, ancient sites, churches and galleries may be subject to random periods of closure. The following is just a guide.

Monday is the usual closing day for most monuments, museums and galleries and on any given day some lesser-visited attractions may close earlier than advertised.

Some churches, even quite well-known ones, are shut at all times except for Mass on Sunday or on their saint's day. Most other churches are open in the mornings and late afternoons.

Some saints' feast days are celebrated as holidays and, again, many attractions will be closed at those times. If you find yourself in Rome on these dates, try to visit the major churches of the saint concerned where special services, processions and even feasts are sometimes held. In August many attractions are closed.

Epiphany. 6 January.
Good Friday. Procession to the Colosseum.
St Joseph (S. Giuseppe). 19 March.
St John (S. Giovanni). 23 and 24 June.
St Peter (S. Pietro). 29 June.
Festa della Madonna della Neve. S. Maria Maggiore. 5 August.
   White dahlia petals fall from the roof of the church in memory of a miraculous fall of snow.
Feast of the Assumption. Ferragosto. 15 August. Rome comes to a standstill.
All Saints. 1 November.
S. Stefano. 26 December.

Accademia Nazionale di San Luca, Mon., Wed., Fri. and last
Sun. of month 10.00–13.00.

Ara Pacis Lungotevere. Tues.–Sat. 9.00–16.30 (summer 18.30).
Sun. and holidays 9.00–13.00.

Barracco Museum Tues.–Sat. 9.00–19.00. Sun. and holidays
9.00–13.00.

Baths of Caracalla Tues.–Sat. 9.00–16.00 (summer
9.00–18.00). Mon., Sun. and holidays 9.00–13.00.

Baths of Diocletian (Museo Nazionale Romano) Viale Enrico
de Nicola 79. 9.00–19.45. Closed Monday.

Battelli di Roma (Boat trips on the Tiber)
www.battellidiroma.it. From Tiber Island, Calata degli
Anguillara, frequently from 8.00–19.00.

Borghese Gallery Tues.–Sun. 9.00–19.00. Book in advance.
www.galleriaborghese.it

Botanic Gardens (Trastevere) Tues.–Sat. Sept.–July. 9.30–18.30.

Capitoline Museums Tues.–Sat. 9.00–19.00.

Capuchin Cemetery (in crypt of S. Maria della Concezione,
Via Veneto 27) Fri.–Wed. 9.00–12.00, 15.00–18.00.

Casina delle Civette Villa Torlonia, Via Nomentana. 9.00–
one hour before sunset daily.

For concert tickets: Cooperativa Sogno Viale Regina
Margherita; 06–85 30 17 58, fax: 06–85 30 17 56, email:
ilsogno@romeguide.it

Castel S. Angelo Tues.–Sun. 9.00–20.00 (summer Tues.–Fri.
9.00–22.00, Sat. 9.00–23.00).

Catacombs of S. Agnese Via Nomentana. 9.00–12.00,
16.00–18.00. Closed Monday p.m. and public holidays.

Catacombs of S. Callisto 8.30–12.00, 16.00–18.00. Closed
Wednesday.

Catacombs of Priscilla Via Salaria. 14.30–17.00 (summer
8.30–12.00, 16.00–18.00). Closed Monday.

Catacombs of S. Sebastiano Via Appia. 8.30–12.30,
14.30–17.30. Closed Thursday.

Colosseum Mon.–Sat. 9.00–15.00 (summer 9.00–19.00) Sun.
and holidays 9.00–13.00.

Convent of S. Cecilia in Trastevere (Cavallini frescoes) Tues. and Thurs. 10.00–11.30, Sun. 11.30–12.00.

Crypta Balbi Tues.–Sun. 9.00–19.45.

Domus Aurea (Nero's Golden House) 9.00–19.45. Book in advance. Closed Tuesday.

Goethe's House Wed.–Mon. 10.00–18.00.

Keats–Shelley Memorial Museum Mon.–Fri. 9.00–13.00, 15.00–18.00, Sat. 11.00–14.00, 15.00–18.00.

MACRO (Museum of Contemporary Art) Tues.–Sat. 10.00–13.30, 14.30–17.30, Sun. 9.30–12.30 (at Via Reggio Emilia 54, off Via Nomentana, and at Piazza Orazio Giustiniani, Testaccio).

Montemartini Art Collection Via Ostiense 106. Tues.–Sun. 9.30–19.00.

Museum of the Dead Souls Lungotevere Prati. Mon.–Sat. 7.30–11.00, 14.30–19.00. **Free**.

Museum of Rome (Palazzo Braschi) Tues.–Sat. 9.00–19.00, Sun. 9.00–13.00.

Museum of the Walls Porto S. Sebastiano. Tues.–Sat. 9.00–19.00. Sun. and holidays 9–13.00.

Museum of Musical Instruments Tues.–Sun. 8.30–19.30.

Museum of the Synagogue Mon.–Thurs. 9.00–16.30 (summer 9.00–19.30) Fri. until noon.

Museum of Trastevere Tues.–Sun. 10.00–20.00.

Palazzo Altemps (National Museum of Rome) Tues.–Sun. 9.00–19.45.

Palazzo Spada Tues.–Sun. 9.00–19.00.

Palazzo Colonna Sat. 9.00–13.00.

Palatine Hill Mon.–Sat. 9.00–15.00 (summer 9.00–18.00).

Protestant Cemetery 9.00–16.30 (summer 9.00–17.00). Closed Monday.

Roman Forum Mon.–Sat. 9.00–15.00 (summer 9.00–18.00). Sun. and holidays 9.00–13.00. **Free**.

Rose Garden of Rome April–July and in October. 8.00–18.30. **Free**.

Tomb of Cecilia Metella Via Appia. Tues.–Sat. 9.00–16.00.

Trajan's Markets Tues.–Sun. 9.00–16.30 (summer 9.00–18.30).

Vatican Museums Mon.–Sat. 8.45–13.45 (high summer and Easter 8.45–16.00). Closed Sundays.

Villa Giulia (Etruscan Museum) Tues.–Sun. 8.30–19.00.

Villa Farnesina (Trastevere) Mon.–Sat. 9.00–13.00.

Waxworks (Museo delle Cere) Daily. 9.00–20.00.

TOURIST INFORMATION

Tourist information kiosks
Daily, 9.30–19.30.
Castel Sant'Angelo – Piazza Pia
Fontana di Trevi – Via Minghetti
Fori Imperiali – Piazza del Tempio della Pace
Navona – Piazza delle Cincque Lune
Santa Maria Maggiore – Via dell'Olmata
Stazione Termini – Piazza dei Cinquecento and opposite
    Platform 4
Piazza S. Giovanni in Laterano

Wanted in Rome, sold in English bookshops (Via del Moro, Trastevere, Via della Vite and Via dei Greci, Spanish Steps, etc.), also has extensive listings for theatre, concerts, opera and exhibitions, reviews and small ads.

www.whatsoninrome.com is an excellent website run for the English-speaking community in Rome with up-to-date listings and other interesting articles.

PUBLIC TRANSPORT

Much of Rome is easily covered on foot, in many cases more easily than by sitting in traffic in a bus or taxi.

The underground Metro trains are limited in range. Tickets need to be bought at the station and franked as you go onto the platform.

Tickets for buses and trams have to be bought before you travel and have to be franked as you start your journey. They are on sale at bars and tobacconists with a sign outside. BIG are integrated tickets that provide a day's travel on all public transport (excluding trips to Fiumcino airport).

Destinations are clearly marked at each bus or tram stop and the Roma Metro-Bus Map, available at most news-stands, is invaluable.

Taxi ranks are fairly well distributed and are marked on many maps. This is the easiest way to take one, although they can sometimes be hailed successfully on the street. Only use official yellow taxis with a TAXI sign on the vehicle's roof.

HOTELS

There are many excellent hotels in Rome. What follows is a personal selection of establishments that offer something extra in terms of position, historic associations, amenity or atmosphere compared with others in their class or price range.

*indicates hotels of extra charm or in a particularly good location.

EXPENSIVE

La Russie (Spanish Steps) Via del Babuino 9: +39 06 32 88 81 Fax: +39 06 32 88 88 88 email: reservations@hotelderussie.it
***Raphael** (Piazza Navona) Lago Febo 2: +39 06 68 28 31
Minerve Grand (Pantheon) Piazza Della Minerva 39: +39 06 69 52 01
Aldrovandi Palace (Borghese Gardens) Via Aldrovandi 5: +39 06 32 23 993 (swimming pool)
Columbus (Vatican) Via della Conciliazione 33: +39 06 68 65 435

MIDDLING

***Hotel Santa Maria** (Trastevere) Vicolo del Piede 2: +39 06 58 94 626 fax: +39 06 58 94 815
***Art** (Spanish Steps) Via Margutta 56: +39 06 32 87 11 email: hotelart@slh.com
Sole al Pantheon (Pantheon) Piazza della Rotonda 63: +39 06 67 80 441
Dei Borgognoni (Spanish Steps) Via del Bufalo: +39 06 69 94 15 05

Residenze Farnese (Campo de' Fiori) Via del Mascherone 59: +39 06 68 89 13 88

Casa di Santa Brigida (Campo de' Fiori) Piazza Farnese 96: +39 06 68 89 25 96

S. Anselmo (Aventine) Piazza S. Anselmo 2: +39 06 57 43 547

Capo d'Africa (Colosseum) Via Capo d'Africa 54: +39 06 77 28 01

Stendhal Hotel (Spanish Steps) Via del Tritone 113: +39 06 42 29 21 fax: +39 06 42 29 255

***Domus Aventino** (Aventine) Via di S. Prisca 11: +39 06 57 46 135

Hotel St George Via dei Bresciani 36 (angolo Via Giulia): +39 06 68 66 11

MODERATE

***Portoghesi** (North of Piazza Navona) Via dei Portoghesi 1: +39 06 68 64 231

Campo di Fiori (Campo de' Fiori) Via del Biscione 6: +39 06 68 80 68 65

Santa Chiara (Pantheon) Via Santa Chiara 21: +39 06 68 72 979

Hotel Celio (Colosseum) Via dei S. Quattro Coronati 35: +39 06 70 49 53 33

***Trastevere House** (Trastevere) Vicolo del Buco 7: +39 06 58 83 774

San Francesco (Trastevere/Porto Portese) Via Jacopa de' Settesoli 7: +39 06 58 33 34 13

Hotel della Conciliazone (Vatican) Borgo Pio 163: +39 06 68 79 10

***Teatro di Pompeo** (Campo de' Fiori) Largo del Pallaro 8: +39 06 68 72 812

Hotel Cisterna (Trastevere) Via della Cisterna 7–9: +39 06 58 17 212

Hotel Trevi (Trevi Fountain) Vicolo dei Babuccio 21: +39 06 67 89 563

Domus Tiberina (Trastevere) Via in Piscinula 37: +39 06 58 03 033

Hotel Adriano (Piazza Navona) Via di Pallacorda 2: +39 06 68 80 24 51

B&B

Filomena e Francesca (Vatican) Via della Giuliana 72: +39 06 37 51 36 25 *www.bhrhotels.com*

RESTAURANTS

* = restaurants of exceptional charm, service, location or value.
! = top-class restaurants, usually more expensive.

Roman restaurants are often closed on either Sunday or, more frequently, Monday, but there are exceptions (see below).

Grotte del Teatro di Pompeo (Campo de' Fiori) Via del Biscione, 73: +39 06 68 80 36 86. Closed Monday.

Al Pompiere (Ghetto) Via S. Maria dei Calderari: +39 06 68 68 377. Traditional Romano-Jewish food.

Osteria da Nerone (Colosseum) Via delle Terme di Tito 96. Closed Sunday.

Miro (Ponte S. Angelo) Via dei Banchi Nuovi 8: +39 06 68 80 85 27. Calabrian food.

Filetti di Baccala (Campo de' Fiori) Largo dei Librari 88. In essence, fish and chips.

! Il Pagliaccio (Campo de' Fiori) Via dei Banchi Vecchi 129a: +39 06 68 80 95 95.

Perilli (Testaccio) Via Marmorata 39: +39 06 57 42 415. Traditional Roman food; 100-year-old interior.

Antica Taverna Via Monte Giordano 12: +39 06 68 80 10 53. Open every day.

Vinando (Ghetto) Piazza Margana 23: +39 06 69 20 07 41. Wine bar with food.

Hostaria Antica Roma (Appian Way) Via Appia Antica 87: +39 06 51 32 888.

Caffetteria DART (Piazza Navona) Cloister Bramante, Via della Pace: +39 06 68 80 90 35.

! Al Presidente (Trevi Fountain) Via in Arcione 95: +39 06 67 97 342. Closed Monday.

* *La Taverna degli Amici* (Ghetto) Piazza Margana 36–7: +39 06 69 92 06 37. Closed Monday.

! Sora Lelle (Tiber Island) Via Ponte Quattro Capi 16: +39 06 68 61 601. Closed Sunday.

Enoteca Constantini (Vatican) Piazza Cavour 16: +39 06 32 11 502. Wine, and food chosen to accompany it. Closed Sunday.

Da Baffetto (Piazza Navona) Via del Governo Vecchio 114. Pizza. Open every day.

Margutta Vegetariano (Spanish Steps) Via Margutta 118: +39 06 32 65 77. Vegetarian. Open every day.

Ristorante Giulio (Campo de' Fiori) Via della Barchetta 19: +39 06 88 06 466. Closed Sunday.

! Ristorante Papagio (Colosseum) Via Capo d'Africa 26: +39 06 70 09 800. Fish.

Da Giggetto (Ghetto) Via del Porto D'Ottavia 21–2: +39 06 68 61 105. Jewish cuisine. Closed Monday.

Augusturello (Testaccio) Via G. Branca 98: +39 06 57 46 585. Traditional Roman offal dishes. Closed Sunday.

Surya Mahal (Trastevere) Piazza Trilussa 50: +39 06 58 94 554. Indian food. Closed Sunday.

! Alberto Ciarla (Trastevere) Piazza di S. Cosimato 40: +39 06 58 18 668. Fish. Closed Sunday.

!Vecchia Roma (Ghetto) Piazza Campitelli 18: +39 06 68 64 604. Closed Wednesday.

Le Scale Parione (Campo de' Fiori) Via dei Cappellari 74: +39 06 68 30 95 30. Closed Tuesday.

Terre di Siena (Piazza Navona) Piazza Pasquino: +39 06 68 30 77 04. Tuscan cooking.

La Mandragola Via dell' Orso 71: +39 06 68 34 030.

La Rotonda (Villa Borghese) Via Livenza 7: +39 06 88 42 171. Dinner in a thirteenth-century farmhouse.

Velando (Vatican) Borgo Vittorio 26: +39 06 68 80 99 55. Cooking from Val Camonica, N. Italy. Closed Sunday.

La Tana di Noantri (Trastevere) Via Paglia1: +39 06 58 06 404. Closed Tuesday.

Le Coppedé (Nomentana) Via Taro 28: +39 06 84 11 772. Cooking from Apulia in Art Nouveau-style house, typical of the area. Closed Sunday.

! Checchino dal 1880 (Testaccio) Via di Monte Testaccio: +39 06 57 46 318. Closed Sunday and Monday.

Colline Emiliane (Piazza Barberini) Via degli Avignonesi 22: +39 06 48 17 538. Bolognese cuisine. Closed Fridays.

!Taverna Angelica (Vatican/Prati) Piazza A. Capponi 6: +39 06 68 74 514. Open every day.

FURTHER READING

The following is a very small selection of books which I have found invaluable in my own continuing discovery of Rome.

The Museo Nazionale Romano publishes a collection of beautifully illustrated, slender volumes, translated into several languages, on each of its major monuments. These are widely available at museums. The tourist office's leaflets on subjects as diverse as medieval churches, the bridges of the Tiber and small squares in Rome are excellent. These are free from any tourist information office (see listings).

For an understanding of ancient Rome as history written in stone and brick, and for the ability to make sense of the disparate, and sometimes overwhelming, legacy of ruins and the culture which created them, Amanda Claridge's *Rome* in the Oxford Archaeological guides series, is without equal. I have been indebted to it again and again. On the Colosseum, Keith Hopkins' and Mary Beard's newly published *Colosseum* is a wide-ranging exploration of the long life and extraordinary cultural flexibility of Rome's most iconic building, written with the insight and wit one might expect from these authors.

Matilda Webb's *The Churches and Catacombs of Early Rome* is clear, intelligent and arranged in interesting itineraries, while David Mayernik has some clever and imaginatively written chapters on Rome in his book *Timeless Cities: An Architect's Reflections on Renaissance Italy*.

A meditation on just one building, S. Agnese Fuori le

Mura, with a breadth of information about the whole period, Marguerite Visser's *Geometry of Love* is unusual and beautifully achieved.

For the complexities of the war years and its heritage, read Robert Katz's *The Battle for Rome: The Germans, the Allies, the Partisans, and the Pope, September 1943–June 1944*.

For a broad view, Georgina Masson's *The Companion Guide to Rome* has been without equal for forty years. It is revised frequently. Another stalwart is *Rome: A Literary Companion* by John Varriano.

Food lovers should try and obtain *Roma del Gambero Rosso*, the guide to restaurants used by Romans themselves and sold at most news-stands in the city. It is easy to read, includes a dictionary and is a remarkably pleasant way to improve one's Italian as well as one's diet.

Carlo Levi (1902–75) was a Roman writer, painter and politician. *Fleeting Rome* is a newly translated collection of his wonderful essays about the city and, above all, the lives, passions and eccentricities of the people he loved.

Finally, for a very entertaining read – intelligent, scrupulously detailed, written with love, prejudice and respect, and still remarkably relevant – the great classic is Augustus Hare's *Walks in Rome*, first published in 1872.

INDEX

Numbers in italics refer to illustrations.

Thus the whole circle of travellers may be reduced to the following *Heads*.

Idle Travellers
Inquisitive Travellers
Lying Travellers
Proud Travellers
Vain Travellers
Splenetic Travellers.

Then follow the travellers of Necessity.

The delinquent and felonious Traveller
The unfortunate and innocent Traveller
The simple Traveller.

And last of all (if you please) The Sentimental Traveller (meaning thereby myself) who have travell'd, and of which I am now sitting down to give an account – as much out of *Necessity* . . . as any one in the class.

Laurence Sterne, *The Sentimental Traveller* (1768)